Dynasty: A Very Short Introduction

VERY SHORT INTRODUCTIONS are for anyone wanting a stimulating and accessible way into a new subject. They are written by experts, and have been translated into more than 45 different languages.

The series began in 1995, and now covers a wide variety of topics in every discipline. The VSI library currently contains over 600 volumes—a Very Short Introduction to everything from Psychology and Philosophy of Science to American History and Relativity—and continues to grow in every subject area.

Very Short Introductions available now:

Available soon:

For more information visit our website

www.oup.com/vsi/

Jeroen Duindam

DYNASTY

A Very Short Introduction

OXFORD
UNIVERSITY PRESS

OXFORD
UNIVERSITY PRESS

Great Clarendon Street, Oxford, OX2 6DP,
United Kingdom

Oxford University Press is a department of the University of Oxford.
It furthers the University's objective of excellence in research, scholarship,
and education by publishing worldwide. Oxford is a registered trade mark of
Oxford University Press in the UK and in certain other countries

First edition published in 2019

Impression: 1

Published in the United States of America by Oxford University Press
198 Madison Avenue, New York, NY 10016, United States of America

British Library Cataloguing in Publication Data

Data available

Library of Congress Control Number: 2019946098

ISBN 978-0-19-880908-1

Printed in Great Britain by
Ashford Colour Press Ltd, Gosport, Hampshire

Contents

Acknowledgements

The Leiden Institute for History allowed me to concentrate on writing a first draft of this book in the spring semester of 2017–18. Students of my Leiden graduate seminar on dynasties in the first semester of 2018–19 suggested several improvements. I wish to thank friends and colleagues who commented on this book in various stages of its genesis: Hans van Eenennaam, Raymond Fagel, Kirstin Kleber, Roel Kraaijenbrink, Lloyd Llewellyn-Jones, Gjovalin Macaj, Walter Pohl, Hamish Scott, Petra Sijpesteijn, Quinten Somsen, Jasper van der Steen, Alan Strathern, Rolf Strootman, Marija Wakounig, and Joost Welten.

Anonymous OUP reviewers provided helpful comments; I particularly thank Andrea Keegan and Jenny Nugee for their advice and support. Joy Mellor and Dorothy McCarthy carefully corrected my text and suggested several improvements. Kate Delaney, my long-standing friend and editor, again offered invaluable help. Finally, my wife Mariella and my sons Guus and Nol all contributed in various ways to this result.

List of illustrations

Dynasties past and present

Royal dynasties enjoy a mixed reputation. Enlightened opinion associates traditional royalty with militant triumphalism, despotism, pomp, squandering, ineptitude, and corruption. Only a handful of nostalgists dream about the restoration of kings and queens; modern variants of dynastic power are regarded with suspicion or, at best, insouciance. Yet at the same time, biographies about individual princes or princesses find an eager public, and royalty is ubiquitous in celebrity gossip magazines. Royal deaths, births, marriages, and coronations draw crowds and glue numerous others to their TV screens. The charm of royalty pervades popular fiction and entertainment. Dynastic conquerors perform their violent feats in computer games; the struggles among competing houses inspire TV series. Even without the charisma of royalty, dynasties abound in the entertainment industry, with soaps about rivalling business houses and shows about celebrity families.

This continuing fascination should not come as a surprise: families are a fact of life in all times and places. Only in the last two centuries, moreover, did conspicuous royal families gradually recede from the heart of power. Kings, queens and their families have pervaded world history from the moment humankind started to plant fields, tame animals, build cities, and raise taxes. Under many names and titles, the royal formula prevailed worldwide during at least five millennia, from small scriptless chiefdoms to colossal bureaucratic empires. Lone figures elevated to a dignity that surpassed everyday standards and at times approximated the divine became copestones of hierarchical societies. Throughout world history men were seen as the natural candidates for paramount rule, but in circumstances that will be discussed at length below women rose to power—and they were always present behind the throne. Kings were inevitably connected to a family: rulers cherished their forebears, groomed their successors, and warily surveyed their relatives. The logic of family and heredity was accepted even by outsiders who ascended the throne through violent action. These newcomers invented connections to previous ruling houses and were keen to transmit power to their offspring. Kingship invariably engendered dynasty.

A dynasty is a family of kings, the king an inflated variant of the everyday family father. Royal dynasties magnify common tribulations of family life; they present all human appetites, weaknesses, and strengths in overstated form. Among dynastic relatives, rivalry was more likely than affection. The heroism, blunders, and idiosyncrasies of kings and their troubled families have moved many pens. Chronicles from around the globe narrate the lives and deeds of kings; modern biographies provide ample detail about royalty in past and present. Paradoxically, while the histories of many individual kings are well-known, the collective history of kingship and dynasty remains a *terra incognita*.

Specialists hesitate to cross accepted boundaries of space and time. Archaeologists, historians, art historians, anthropologists, and sociologists, to name but the most likely disciplines, have looked at dynastic history with diverging methods and purposes. Archaeologists and art historians primarily examine artefacts, historians primarily study texts, yet they all usually focus on a limited period and area; few scholars have ventured to bring together widely dispersed examples. While anthropologists have examined the recurring importance of dynasty, kinship, succession, and mythology in diverse settings, their research primarily dealt with small 'primitive' societies, distant from the mores and concerns of the world's dominant script cultures. Conversely, most historians have focused on 'Western civilization': sustained intellectual engagement among Europeanists and specialists studying the languages, cultures, and histories of other script cultures has remained surprisingly limited. Sociologists, finally, have tended to concentrate on modern societies; in their work, dynastic rule figures mostly as a stage in the development towards political modernity. Contrasts between these disciplines have been fading, in terms of traditional areas of study as well as in methods. Nevertheless, no single overarching view of dynasty and kingship is available in the literature.

This book examines the shared history of rulers and their families worldwide, from the first empires using written documentation to the French Revolution. It then considers the persistence of the dynastic impulse in the modern world, and invites readers to view their age through the lens of dynasty. Zooming in on the point where sovereignty and lineage converge, it first and foremost explains the experience of kings, sultans, emperors, and caliphs struggling to establish themselves among their forebears and relatives as well as in the machinery of government. What did figures on the throne during these five millennia of human history hold in common? How can we explain the troubled relationship among dynastic scions? What was the role of women: on the throne, as mothers, spouses, concubines, or daughters? How did regional differences and change over time impact these matters?

Inevitably, the rules of thumb of kingship outlined in the following chapters resonate with leadership in other situations. Can they be read as a guide to success? Recently, an abridged edition of the reflections of a Chinese emperor was marketed as a guidebook for leaders in all settings. Without a doubt, the emperor proffered many wisdoms, yet he did so first and foremost to establish his

3

own reputation. Indeed, most rulers have been keen to underline their own accomplishments rather than divulge the dilemmas inherent in their role. Nevertheless, even embellished memoirs unveil some of the persistent complexities of supreme executive power, and readers will recognize predicaments of modern leadership in the pages of this book. Defining problems was always easier than providing clear-cut solutions. Royal advisors understood that good advice would have to be gauged by the temperament of the leader as much as depending on the issue to be solved: impetuous figures needed to be restrained, indolent characters activated. Harmonious leadership, they concluded, demanded a correct apportioning of responsibilities between the sovereign and his advisors.

Dynasties were never limited to the supreme level of ruling sovereigns: a concern for family status and continuity will be found across the social spectrum. This consideration is relevant for this book in two ways. First, the notion of undivided authority developed only gradually: rulers shared sovereignty not only with their relatives, but also with hereditary elites wielding authority in the regions. Second, many dynasties persisting into the 21st century no longer hold sovereign power, which is now vested in legislative assemblies. Modern political dynasties function on the basis of the popular vote rather than as sovereign families; business tycoons can inherit wealth as well as leadership without ever sharing in sovereign power. Nevertheless, the combination of leadership and family persists, in the business world as well as in politics. Modern-day variants of dynasty occupy centre stage in this book's final chapter.

Family brings to mind reproduction and physical heredity. Dynasty, however, was never only a biological fact. Geneticists may be correct in arguing that sixteen million descendants of the famed Mongol founder Chinggis Khan (1162; r. 1206–27) can be traced in the modern world, yet these distant relatives do not see themselves as Chinggisid scions. Conversely, the genealogies so important for historic ruling houses typically included fanciful additions and connections. Royal power demanded prestigious forebears, even if they needed to be fabricated. Preventing extinction, moreover, entailed frequent manipulation: children were adopted and inserted in the family tree. Dynasty, in short, was always a construction. It was the result of a volatile mixture of cultural rules defining kinship, the vagaries of demography, and the attempt of families to ensure their continuity in power.

The combination between lineage and sovereign power, the core of this book, can be retraced in the history of the word dynasty. Ancient Greek *dynasteia* denoted lordship or sovereignty in general, although the term *dynastes* referred to petty rulers. Aristotle used *dynasteia* to indicate an oligarchy dominated by a handful of families. Only with the 3rd-century-BCE history of Egypt written in Greek by an Egyptian priest, Manetho, do we find 'dynasty' in its current meaning as a line of kings. Manetho conveniently grouped Egyptian kings into a sequence of numbered dynasties. European scholars gradually extended the term to Asian empires from China to Persia. However, ruling families in Europe would be referred to as a 'house': the house of Tudor, the *Haus* Hohenzollern. From the late 18th century onwards dynasty emerged as a synonym for house. Terms related both to sovereign power and to the ruling house can be found in most parts of the world. In West and South Asia, we find *dawla* (Arabic) for dynasty or state; and *khandan* (Persian) for an illustrious family. Chinese *guo* refers to kingdom or country, as in *Zhongguo* (Middle Kingdom), but also to dynasty. It can be found in combination with *chao*, which itself means dynasty, audience, court, and country. Many other terms match the European word 'court', referring to the retinue and abode of a ruler, but also to sovereignty and supreme justice.

Chapter 1
Shaping the family

Male and female lines: concentration versus diffusion?

A dynasty is a line of kings reaching back into the past, yet it also is the extended group of relatives around a living sovereign. Lists of kings register the chain of rulers forming the dynasty across time: the 'vertical' family. At any point in time, rulers keep track of their relatives, the 'horizontal' family. Vertical and horizontal families could be shaped in many ways: depending on ideas about bloodlines, practices of procreation, and rules for succession, dynasties could comprise a handful or thousands.

Fathers and sons dominate in kinglists: we usually understand a dynasty as a continuing line of fathers succeeded by their sons, punctuated incidentally by the reign of daughters. The preponderance of males in power can easily obscure the fact that kinship and succession were not invariably reckoned through the male line. An estimated 30 per cent of societies worldwide practised matrilineal descent. These peoples accepted only the mother's blood and womb as the carrier of kinship: children belonged to their mother's, rather than to their father's, families. Succession through the female line did not affect the common preference for males as supreme power holders, but it profoundly altered the notion of dynasty. There would still be lines of kings and families in power, but sons were now barred from succeeding their fathers. Straight 'downwards' father–son continuity was possible only in the case of incestuous unions—sons sired by kings and women lacking royal blood held no rights to the throne. Therefore, candidates for succession needed to be found 'sideways', among offspring of the king's female relatives, most often his maternal brothers or the sons of his sisters. Matrilineal succession entailed choice, competition, and diffusion of power.

Matrilineality was markedly present in Africa. In the north, the Saharan Tuareg and other Berber-speaking tribes traced sovereignty through the female line. West Africa counted a number of matrilineal kingdoms, most famously the Asante federation (1670–1896). Bantu migration south-eastward across Sub-Saharan Africa created a belt of matrilineal polities between the Niger-Congo area and Zambia. In South-West India and Sri Lanka more examples can be found. Matrilineality seems to have been dominant in the early history of Austronesia, the region connecting the South-East Asian archipelago with Polynesia and Madagascar. The Jewish Rabbinic law, stipulating that in a mixed marriage the mother's status defines that of the children, is perhaps the most familiar instance of matrilineality. Jewish royal dynasties, however, followed patrilineal succession. Concentrated outside of the temperate climate zones, and largely restricted to smaller-scale horticultural societies, matrilineal succession has gradually been pushed back during recent centuries. Colonial regimes in Africa found it difficult to deal with the intricacies of succession in their territories, and promoted familiar European rules predicated on male next-of-kin succession. In North Africa, the impact of Islam and the migration of Arab pastoralists had long since pushed in the same direction.

The downwards continuity of the dynastic line through father–son succession in principle fosters concentration of power; in practice violent competition among sons and other male relatives has often torn apart ruling families and fragmented their domains.

In the long run, rulers of larger kingdoms and empires tried to consolidate their realm by stipulating its indivisibility and prearranging the priority of succession, usually by defining the first-born son as sole heir. Male primogeniture prevented strife and concentrated political power in the royal line, advantages which made it the dominant form of succession in recent history.

However, the concentration of power and wealth engendered by unbroken dynastic continuity was not universally seen as desirable. Many patrilineal polities in Africa prohibited the succession of the king's eldest son, or all sons of a ruling king. Such prohibitions invited competition because they left open a number of candidates without predetermined priority. Bloody succession contests could ravage kingdoms, but they had several advantages. All potential candidates were required to canvass for support and seek the endorsement of elites and leading officeholders. More than fixed next-of-kin succession, competition among eligibles made possible the ascent of qualified contenders with an eye for the needs of their constituencies. Moreover, the multiple contestants could be united around the throne by the anticipation of their chance to rise to power. Kingship was expected to change hands—between individuals, between branches of the same family, sometimes between different families or even between segments of society. As long as violence remained limited in duration and scope, open succession could foster integration through political participation.

While patrilineal succession can be either open or closed, matrilineal succession is necessarily open rather than closed, sideways rather than downwards, and based on the principle of diffusion rather than on concentration of power. In the Asante federation, matrilineality went together with strong popular participation and a well-developed tradition of 'destooling' unjust and immoral kings. It reminded the British anthropologist Rattray of Greek democracy. Paramount power in the end was vested in a single person, but the process of acquiring and performing kingship involved many others. The example of matrilineality and the wider practice of diffuse succession fit awkwardly into the neat categories of government by one, by few, or by many. Typically, dynastic kingship included elements of monarchy as well as aristocracy, and sometimes even democracy. Conversely, as we shall see, modern forms of leadership retain many dynastic characteristics.

Heredity was close to the heart of dynastic power, yet outsiders often determined who would be king: the role of such 'kingmakers' could approach full-blown election. Elective thrones, indeed, can be encountered throughout Europe, Africa, and Central Asia. There were limitations: eligibility was most often restricted to the royal descent group, and the kingmakers, too, formed a circumscribed elite. In Africa, kingmakers were as a rule not themselves eligible: this very fact entitled them to act as arbiters. In the Kingdom of Bunyoro, in current Uganda, the first-born son of the king was deprived of the right to succeed, which qualified him to point out a successor among the other members of the royal clan. Kingmaking could take many shapes. Machiavelli was struck by the election of the Mamluk Sultans in Cairo (1250–1517) and compared it to the choice of Roman pontiffs: a new sultan was chosen from among the ranks of elite soldiers; the pope from among the cardinals in the curia. In both cases, moreover, heredity played a role: several families managed to have their scions elected more than once. A mixture of heredity and acclamation prevailed in most kingdoms. The Mongol chiefs assembled in their council (*kurultai*) to elect or confirm a new great khan, and similar councils persisted in the Mongol successor-empires. Peers confirmed the succession of kings in medieval Europe. In England and France, their acclamation retained its ceremonial functions while kingship was defined increasingly through next-of-kin succession. Conversely, in the Holy Roman Empire, the heart of continental Europe, elections became the norm. Three spiritual and four worldly electors (see Figure 1) chose the king of the empire, opening the way for his coronation

1. **The seven electors of the Holy Roman Empire (14th century) choose Henry, Count of Luxembourg, as King of the Romans at Frankfurt on the 27th day of November 1341 (Landeshauptarchiv Koblenz).**

as emperor by the pope. The Habsburgs acquired a *de facto* monopoly on the imperial dignity from the 15th century onwards, but Europe's leading royal houses could step forward as candidates, and the Bavarian house of Wittelsbach briefly occupied this highest dignity of Europe in 1742–5. In Sweden and Denmark elective kingship was replaced by heredity in the 16th and 17th centuries, a pattern also followed in Hungary and Bohemia. Poland, on the other hand, strengthened its tradition of election, which persisted until the final partition of the country in 1795.

Succession patterns had consequences for the choice of partners and for royal reproduction. In patrilineal dynasties the rank of royal spouses could make a difference: their pedigree added prestige to the royal house and they were duly inserted into royal genealogies. Continuity and succession, however, were determined by the male line. Slave concubines in the Ottoman harem, of indifferent background, highlighted the exclusive significance of the House of Osman: here only fatherhood mattered for dynastic legitimacy. Conversely, by defining descent exclusively through the mother, matrilineal succession made irrelevant the male progenitor. This created complications because males were still expected to be the dominant actors in the family: a father might claim authority over his wife and son. Matrilineal princesses could prevent this hazard in two ways: by hiding the identity of their lovers, or by openly having many lovers. Sexual licentiousness made it impossible to pinpoint the father of a royal heir and thus forestalled his undesirable pretensions to power. In addition, it freed princesses from the duty of treating their male partners with subservience and so confirmed their hierarchical supremacy.

In its purest form, dynastic blood required the unison of male and female royals. Breaking the taboo on incest is a common occurrence in myths and cosmologies, whence it travelled to royalty. What was practised by Isis and Osiris or Zeus and Hera was ascribed to royals. Royal genealogies in Hawaii and among the Inca stipulate double royal pedigree, or royal incest, as ideal, although we cannot be sure whether it was ever more than an exception. In ancient Egypt dynastic brother–sister marriages can be found, yet the siblings were often related through only one parent, and some of them may have been adopted—patterns repeated in many other realms. The better-documented proliferation of sibling marriage in Ptolemaic Egypt (305–30 BCE) first and foremost reflected political strategy, and the marital alliances were not necessarily consummated. Famously, Cleopatra VII (69, r. 51–30 BCE) married two brothers before she had an affair with Caesar and a marriage with Mark Antony; and only the two Roman liaisons produced children. Yet instances of royal incest occurred in real life as well as in myth. Maselekwane

Modjadji (r. 1800–54), the first of six 'rain queens' ruling Lovedu (South Africa), allegedly acquired her fabled rainmaking skills because she was born from the incestuous union of her father with another daughter.

Matrilineality alerts us to sideways succession and its crucial impact on dynasty. Yet it also uncovers patterns of dynastic rivalry and alliance. Patrilineal dynasties show permanent contestation between agnates. Succession rights strained the relations of kings with their paternal uncles, brothers, and sons. In matrilineal settings, however, these relatives became the king's steadfast supporters: they could not succeed to the throne and their hopes of advancement now depended first and foremost on the royal bounty. Conversely, the king's relationship with maternal relatives would be tenser. In addition, marriage alliances changed form: kings' sons could only hope to see their offspring on the throne by marrying female royals. Male princes now adopted the position typically held by princesses elsewhere, as *traits d'union* between the bloodlines. Matrilineality highlights the flexibility of gender roles, the tensions engendered by succession rights, and the relevance of alliances through the male as well as the female lines—key themes for the study of kingship and dynasty.

Polygyny and monogamy

Patrilineal succession predominated in history; moreover, matrilineality was gradually pushed back even in regions where it used to be strong: Africa and Austronesia. A far more outspoken regional contrast appears once we consider royal reproduction: the European exception of dynastic succession through monogamous marriage.

Kings had numerous wives. Polygamy (*poly*=many; *gamos*=marriage) was accepted in principle almost universally, although in practice 'poor men were monogamists all over the world': only the well-to-do could afford to have several wives, kings more than all others. Polygamy almost exclusively refers to one man having multiple women, therefore it can better be called polygyny (*poly*=many; *gyne*=wives). The marriage of one woman with a number of men, polyandry (*poly*=many; *andros*=man), was exceedingly rare, and occurred only side-by-side with polygyny. In fact it was often a practical response to the shortage of women on the marriage market, drained by the powerful and rich who gathered numerous spouses. As a consequence, several single men, often brothers, might choose to live with one woman. The logic that royal status requires multiple sex partners was accepted by ruling queens: some practised polyandry, whereas others redefined themselves as males and assembled girls as concubines. Warrior-queen Nzinga (1583, r. 1624–63) of Ndongo-Matamba (current Angola) started out with the first and continued with the second.

The Arabic term *harem*, with its associations of an inner sanctum inaccessible to most, has been used more generally for the assemblage of palace women providing sexual services. The numbers of women around rulers could reach hundreds, thousands, perhaps even tens of thousands. Huge harems demonstrated royal fertility, virility, and wealth, and therefore numbers may have been wildly overstated. Abu'l Fazl, the official voice of Mughal Emperor Akbar (1542, r. 1556–1605), stated that 5,000 women lived in the harem. However, the Spanish Jesuit father Antonio Monserrate, tutoring one of Akbar's sons, spoke about 300 women, and at the same time remarked that the emperor had only three sons and two daughters. Numbers may have been exaggerated in travellers' reports as well as in royal chronicles. Travel stories about the debauchery of Eastern princes confirmed European expectations of oriental despotism, and at the same time excited the imagination of readers. Large female communities present in palaces around the globe served as schools and workshops, and in some respects resembled nunneries: most women present would never be touched by the prince. Nevertheless, polygyny changed the parameters of dynastic reproduction.

Recruitment of concubines took different shapes: girls were bought in the slave market, captured in warfare, or paid as tribute to a conquering ruler. Alternatively, elite families voluntarily sent daughters to the court as a token of respect and obedience, or levies were organized to select girls from certain favoured groups. Entry into the harem could be coerced or voluntary: women were kept there as hostages safeguarding the loyalty of subjected elites, and as the hope of their families for a brighter future—concubines could rise to become the mother of the next king. Moreover, women did not necessarily stay in the harem: 'retiring' concubines or the daughters born to harem women were given in marriage to elites.

Only in Christian Europe do we find the gradual emergence of monogamous marriage as the norm for legitimate dynastic reproduction and succession. Coptic Christianity did not prevent the Solomonid kings of Ethiopia from having multiple wives; neither did the conversion to Christianity of King João I of Congo in 1491 readily establish monogamous marriage. In Europe the imposition of the norm has been pictured as the outcome of a protracted battle between priests and warriors in the 11th and 12th centuries. The long and troubled history of missionaries convincing African kings to drop polygyny suggests some of the complications of this confrontation. The outcome was hardly conclusive in Europe. Royals may have tried strenuously to adhere to the new moral dictate, yet the presence of numerous mistresses and bastards in the dynastic record shows that their success was limited. However, the new norm defined as illegitimate those born outside of monogamous marriage and thus reduced the numbers of successors to the throne. Bastards, defined by the growing predominance of monogamous marriage, long played a substantial role around the throne, and some even ascended the throne. In the later 14th century bastards still were able to found the royal houses of Aviz (1385–1580) and Trastámara (1369–1516). In the course of the early modern age, they were less easily accommodated into the dynastic landscape.

There was more at stake here than sexual licence or moral restraint. African kings, pressured by missionaries to drop polygyny, explained that the harem formed the core of a network of political alliances based on the exchange of women. Notwithstanding his conversion to Christianity and his monogamous lifestyle during a protracted exile in the Seychelles, Asante King Prempeh I restored the harem upon his return to the capital city Kumase in 1926: this was the foundation of his state. The proliferation of women around the king was of great importance for the social embedding of rulership.

Queens and empresses at the apex of the harem represented alliances with ruling houses or leading elites. By marrying Persian and Hindu Rajput princesses, Mughal emperors connected these royal families to their court. Daughters and sisters from the patriline were another conduit for dynastic alliances. Neither the daughters of Ottoman sultans nor their offspring could claim succession rights, yet these women tied the echelon of leading officeholders to the ruling house by consistently marrying pashas and viziers. As these dignitaries were often elderly men, who, in addition, frequently faced the sultan's wrath and subsequent execution, marriages tended to be short and could be repeated: two daughters of the formidable Ottoman queen-mother Kösem Sultan (1589–1651) married six and seven times, respectively. Sultanic in-laws (*damads*) and their offspring came to dominate the upper layers of the Ottoman state.

European royals married among leading families in their realms, but from the later Middle Ages onwards increasingly restricted their choice to sovereign houses. Monogamous dynastic intermarriage transformed European royalty into a web of interrelated families, sharing a portfolio of succession rights.

Succession became an international issue: intermarriage spawned pretenders in many countries. Rivalling houses married to celebrate the end of wars, and henceforth found themselves entangled in succession conflict. Erasmus complained that these unions made wars

> more frequent and more frightful. For if kingdoms are linked to another by marriage, whenever one prince is offended he calls in all the rest... for some trifling offence the best part of Christendom is immediately brought to arms.

Gradually, succession was determined on the battlefield more often than in internal upheavals. No part of the globe escaped from succession violence, yet the shape and scale of conflict was determined by the nature of reproduction, succession, and alliances.

Monogamous reproduction reduced the numbers in European royal families. Repeated marriage among the limited number of sovereign houses, moreover, increased chances of extinction, because it tended to reduce fertility and undermine health. The senior line of any European ruling house counted a handful of people; with cadet lines—the sons of younger royal brothers, including earlier generations—numbers doubled or perhaps tripled. Extinction of the senior line was a permanent risk, and the disappearance of the entire house a distinct possibility. At he other extreme of the global spectrum, Chinese imperial clans numbered tens of thousands of princes. One emperor could father as many children as the totals of European senior and junior lines combined: Song Emperor Huizong (1082, r. 1100–26) holds the record with sixty-five children. While extinction remained a possibility here too, a solution was always ready at hand: adopting into the ruling line a suitable prince from among the numerous members of the imperial clan. This method, recurrent in Chinese history, also helps to explain the remarkable longevity of the Japanese imperial house.

The rising numbers of idle princely mouths, prevented from entering regular careers by their birth rank, had marked disadvantages. Paying the stipends of the imperial clan became one of the major burdens of the late Ming government: the princes, themselves practising polygyny, numbered more than 100,000 and perhaps 200,000 by the end of the dynasty. Ming princes were particularly numerous, yet all longer-lasting Chinese dynasties counted the number of princes in tens of thousands. Dynasties worldwide stood between the extremes of diminutive European royal houses and China's huge imperial clans. The diverging numbers had a major impact on the cultural understanding of dynasty, yet they also posed very different challenges for the incumbent rulers trying to effectively govern their families.

Pruning the tree

Elites throughout history have grappled with the challenge of navigating between the Scylla of extinction and the Charybdis of loss of status. How could the horizontal family best be harnessed to secure the continuity of the vertical family? Siring many children guaranteed the continuity of the family, but brought the risk of social decline. Equal partition of land and wealth among all inheritors diluted family status; concentration in the hands of one or few created have-nots within the family. Birth control was used to prevent dilution, but betting on few children increased the threat of extinction. Without the benefit of clairvoyance, every irrevocable choice could jeopardize the family future. Practical solutions were devised to manage risks. Supernumerary boys could enter monasteries and practise celibacy; girls, likewise, could take religious vows or remain unmarried. Boys could resume their responsibility for family continuity after the death of their siblings.

House rules were established to delineate the entitlements of individual members of the family, with the purpose of conserving the patrimony. Equal partible inheritance was the exception among social elites throughout history; most often the shares of daughters were reduced, and inheritance rights could be differentiated for the sons. Everywhere, an office or rank held by the head of the family compounded the problem: who were eligible to succeed to the dignity? Was succession fixed by rigid rules, did the incumbent have the right to designate a successor, was a council of stakeholders consulted? Was the bloodline the main determinant, or could it be overruled by the qualities and dispositions of the candidates? In this case, a test of strength among a wider group of eligibles might decide the outcome. Fixed hereditary succession—most commonly by the eldest son—in no way guaranteed the qualities of the new officeholder. Yet selection by kingmakers or competition through a test of capabilities produced repeated long phases of uncertainty and rivalry. The administrators of a consolidated empire, much like managers of a smoothly run business operation, might prefer a pliable but unremarkable successor over a more talented but less easily swayed family scion. Succession to office in the hands of families shows the same tensions anywhere, but the stakes were highest for the ultimate dignity of kingship.

Between the 14th and the 17th century, the upper layers of the European nobility followed a path that resembled in many ways the simultaneous consolidation of monarchy. Rules for inheritance and succession were altered in favour of first-born sons. The family title as well as the main properties were to remain in the hands of a sequence of eldest sons. This widened the distance between the head of the house and his siblings as well as between senior and junior branches. At the same time family property was protected against the caprices of the family head. The property, or at least an important share of it, could not be alienated or burdened with debts: this was the family trust (*fideicommissum*). Immense landed wealth therefore could go together with a modest budget. Spendthrifts would notice to their dismay that they could consume only a limited share of the family capital. Royal sovereigns likewise could not unreservedly exploit their countries: sovereignty entailed responsibilities and restrictions.

Dynasties differed in their forms of descent and reproduction; yet in all dynasties there were scions who found themselves without a throne. What to do with these royal extras? Was it preferable to prune the dynastic tree or to let it bloom unhampered? Were the rights of princes curtailed? How were they fitted into the dynastic enterprise? The birth rank of princes demanded some near-sovereign occupation: high military command, the government of a province, or a position as advisor. However, trusting these grandees with leading office was fraught with dangers.

Chinese imperial clans showed continued expansion. Weighing the consequences of this proliferation, Tang Taizong (598, r. 626–49) stated that 'a branch can get so heavy that it breaks the trunk; a tail can get too big to be wagged'. The Tang emperor's concerns did not lead to a reduction of the princes, but subsequent dynasties did curtail the rights of imperial clans. Princes were barred from succession and carefully monitored by the government in all dynasties. During the first part of the Song dynasty (960–1279), they were concentrated in the capital and were not expected to enter careers. After the onslaught of the Jurchen Jin dynasty (1115–1234) in the North, rules were relaxed and princes were allowed to enter government. In Ming China (1368–1644), princes resided in the provinces in an enforced otium: they could no longer pass civil service examination or enter government. Qing (1644–1912) princes lived close to Beijing and were employed in imperial government. However, they too were under strict supervision; misdemeanour would be punished by demotion. Succession rights were restricted to the ruling emperor's sons, and the princes were circumscribed in their actions. Overall, the disenfranchisement of princes allowed the unbridled blossoming of the dynastic tree.

At the other extreme stand Turkic and Mongol nomadic steppe dynasties, and their successor-empires in West and South Asia. Sovereign power was viewed here as a quality shared by the clan: no male relative was wholly excluded from succession. Designation by the incumbent khan, confirmation by a council of elders, the voice of the queen-mother, and a preference for the first-born son together formed a volatile formula for succession. These inconsistent criteria paved the way for rebellion; in the end, the military allure of candidates often tipped the balance.

The dynastic tree was cut back radically by repeated and violent contestation. The three Turkic successor-empires of the early modern age, the Safavids, the Mughals, and the Ottomans, followed this tradition in different ways. Safavid shahs upon reaching power habitually blinded fellow-princes, an injury which was seen as irreconcilable with sovereign rule. Mughal princes prepared for battle upon the approach of their father's demise; the victor eradicated his brothers in the process of capturing the throne. The Ottomans systematically practised fratricide (*frater*=brother; *occidere*=kill) in the 15th and 16th centuries: brothers ruling their own provinces were either killed in the scramble for the throne or executed afterward on the authority of the new sultan. In each of these cases, the problem of proliferating junior lines—non-succeeding brothers and their sons—did not emerge. Family violence did at times lead to grumbling in the empire and among its neighbours, notably in 1553 and 1561 when Süleyman had several of his sons executed (filicide: *filius*=son; *occidere*=kill), and in 1595 when Mehmed III ordered nineteen of his brothers as well as a number of pregnant concubines to be killed upon his accession.

In each of these three empires, the practice changed in the course of the 17th century: princes were no longer executed but had to accept severe circumscriptions: they lived under some form of supervision at the centre, and were not allowed to actively engage in government or to beget children. This changeover shows that violent conflict and internment represent subsequent solutions for the same problem: the threat posed by the princes' collective entitlement to dynastic rule. Succession battles and executions took away this difficulty at the price of bloody and unpredictable interregnums. Internment at the centre solved the problem by eliminating the princes' potential for armed revolt. This reduced the danger of nationwide violence, but made the dynasty dependent on contending palace factions. The scions of the House of Osman awaiting their fate in the harem had become pawns in the contests of others, although they could forcefully reclaim power after their enthronement.

The place of princes in dynastic polities can be surmised by asking three questions. How were succession rights delineated? Did princes hold high office? Were they under some form of preventive control? Finally, the location of princes, at the political centre or in the periphery, formed part of the equation. High office in the provinces prepared eligible princes for a violent succession battle; the outcome reduced the dynasty to a single new ruler with his offspring and so radically solved the problem of dynastic extras. Incarceration at the centre emerged as an alternative formula: collective rights of succession made it imperative either to reduce, or to control the princes. Curtailing succession rights, the Chinese way out of the predicament, allowed the growth of the dynastic clan while strictly reserving the throne for the sons and brothers of the incumbent emperor. Yet from Ming to Qing China we can see a change from enforced political inactivity in the periphery to strictly controlled activity at the centre.

In African kingdoms similar patterns can be recognized. The Solomonids of Ethiopia adopted the practice of internment: princes were huddled together on the 'Royal Mountain', where they awaited their fate: accession to the throne or continued confinement. Brothers of the ruling king in Buganda—in present-day Uganda—were allowed to survive in confinement until the birth of a successor, but faced execution or banishment as soon as succession seemed secure. Confinement at the centre, without political or military office, was frequently the lot of princes. In other cases they were sent out to remote areas to fight and govern in the name of the king—distance from the centre neutralized their threat. Exile was the next step: not infrequently, banished royal sons with their supporters created new kingdoms, where they grabbed power and ruled as outsiders. Migrating royals, rising to the throne elsewhere as 'stranger-kings', are a common occurrence in the mythology and history of kingship.

Brothers and sons presented an immediate risk; their offspring could be dealt with in gentler ways, by revoking or simply forgetting their rights. In Buganda only sons of ruling kings were entitled to succession: their offspring lost royal prerogatives and status, and gradually dissolved into the general population. In the small kingdom of Mamprusi (Northern Ghana) drummers documented succession rights by singing the royal genealogy; yet princes who were absent or unable to pay the singers would gradually disappear from the performance.

In subdued form, similar practices appear in Europe. As in China, succession rules became increasingly fixed and restrictive. However, whereas in China princes lost their eligibility for succession, European princes received a place lower down in the hierarchy without forfeiting their rights. Monogamous marriage reduced the number of legitimate candidates and it was frequently necessary to have recourse to these lower-ranking princes. Junior branches of ruling houses were indispensable to prevent succession from moving outward to dynastic rivals across the borders. However, these dynastic juniors tended to be unwieldy subjects.

Members of the Orléans house in France, usually the second-born royal sons with their offspring, represented a challenge for ruling kings. Louis XIII's younger brother Gaston led rebellions; offspring of Louis XIV's younger brother Philippe stepped in as regent for a minor Bourbon king, voted for the execution of another, and finally replaced the last Bourbon king in 1830. They were always the default alternative and therefore rarely entertained a wholly untroubled relationship with the incumbent king. The closer princes were to succession, the more their presence would be experienced as a threat. However, they were also the ideal candidates for missions requiring the prestige of a sovereign. The Habsburgs, ruling in different capacities over many territories, benefited from the service of these royal stand-ins as viceroys, governors, and army commanders. Across Europe, the two patterns seen elsewhere can be found: princes figured at the centre in prestigious surroundings but under the wary eye of their ruling relative, or they were sent out to govern and fight in the periphery of the realm, contributing to the dynastic agenda at a safe distance.

Everywhere princes were a political hazard, yet they were indispensable for dynastic continuity. The circulation of power among a wider group of eligible princes could contribute to internal political cohesion. Conversely, violent competition of princes could give the edge to polities depending on outwards expansion and martial vigour. Most consolidated kingdoms and empires, however, made sure to subject the horizontal family to the requirements of the vertical family: continuity and sovereignty overruled the interests of individual princes.

Chapter 2
Paterfamilias: it's hard to be the boss

Omnipotence and frailty

Kings held responsibility for matters far larger than their lives.
Like the core of a Russian *matryoshka* doll, they were enveloped
by a sequence of outer shells, each representing a higher layer of
responsibility moving from the dynasty and the realm to cosmic
order. These dimensions of royal rule placed considerable
demands on the shoulders of the incumbent. The embellished
deeds of forefathers appeared before novice-kings as a catalogue
of virtues to be imitated. The brightly shining light of their
example raised expectations. Kings needed to maintain order in
their house and preserve the family domains bequeathed to them.
They were expected to learn and respect the traditions of the lands
they governed. Yet their toughest challenge undoubtedly
originated in the divine mandate of kingship.

Titles suggest the connection between royalty and the divine or its
counterpart, the cosmic. Chinese emperors were styled as the 'Son
of Heaven'; caliphs as the 'Shadow of God on Earth'; Persian and
Turco-Mongol rulers as 'Lords of the Auspicious Conjunction'.
Royalty frequently was likened to the sun. The first title of the
Egyptian king was 'Son of Ra' (the Sun god). Hammurabi (1810,
r. 1792–1750 BCE) was depicted as receiving his insignia from the
Sun God, and declared himself to be the 'Sun of the city of

2. Hammurabi (standing) receiving the insignia of power from the Sun God. Hammurabi code, between 1795 and 1750 BCE (Musée du Louvre, Paris).

Babylon, who spreads light over the lands of Sumer and Akkad' (see Figure 2). Japanese emperors were represented as direct descendants of the Sun Goddess Amaterasu. A long line of Sun Kings connects these examples to King Louis XIV of France, who in a 1653 ballet appeared as Apollo. Another among the five titles of the Egyptian king helps us to understand a paradox inherent in kingship: 'he of the Sedge and the Bee'. These symbols of Upper and Lower Egypt also indicated the two faces of the royal status: undying kingship and its ephemeral holder.

More than a century ago, the anthropologist James G. Frazer described in *The Golden Bough* how 'primitive' societies viewed kingship as a sacred quality temporarily bestowed on a human being. Embedding sacredness in a person of flesh and blood demanded endless precautions: the sacred king, 'like a fly in the toils of a spider, could hardly stir a limb for the threads of custom'. Numerous rules elevated kingship, but at the same time circumscribed the movement and contacts of the ruling king. Sacredness could have dramatic consequences. Frazer was particularly struck by the practice of killing kings. Misbehaviour, ailment, or impending death made it necessary to transfer the sacred substance of kingship to another vessel, in other words: to get rid of the king and find a suitable replacement. Regicide (*rex/regis*=king, *occidere*=kill) and enforced suicide recur in myth and history. An example from the relatively recent past illuminates the downsides of sacrality. When in 1880 the barge of Thai Queen Sunanda Kumariratana sank surrounded by baffled onlookers, nobody dared to help the drowning queen: touching sacred royalty was subject to severe punishment.

Throughout Africa it was understood that the health, fertility, and moral stature of kings influenced harvests, weather, and the well-being of the people. Rainmaking skills were attributed to many kings. The stronger the associations of kingship with sacred responsibilities, the more constrained became the life of royals. Sacralized African kings could touch the ground only if it were covered by animal skins, an imperative seriously reducing their mobility. Neither could they communicate directly with their subjects: catching the king's gaze or hearing his voice could wreak havoc—for the transgressor, for the realm, and for the king.

These restrictions were not limited to kings ruling societies traditionally labelled as 'primitive', in Africa and Austronesia. The appropriate performance of rites ranked high among the tasks of Chinese emperors; rainmaking, too, was part of their ritual portfolio. Contacts between the emperor and his subjects were limited to an upper crust of dignitaries, and governed by numerous precautions. Ordinary subjects were not allowed to see the Son of Heaven. There were sound reasons to keep a close watch on the emperor: his personal behaviour, it was thought, could precipitate cosmic disaster—eclipses, droughts, floods—as well as social disorders.

Not all kings were equally sacred. Neither European princes nor West Asian sultans quite matched the untouchable status of some of their fellow kings: they first and foremost held political office and needed to acknowledge the powers of the clergy and Holy Law. Nevertheless, they too mediated between their subjects and divine powers. Umayyad Caliphs (661–750) were seen as empowered to pray for rain. With the Safavids of Iran (1501–1722) and the Mughals of India (1526–1857) the mixture of Islamic, Persian, and Mongol royal traditions obtained a more straightforwardly sacred dimension. Coronation and anointment, it was thought, endowed French and English kings with the power to cure their subjects by touching them. Religion and the sacred were part and parcel of European kingship. In the decades following the restoration of English monarchy in 1660, nearly 100,000 people flocked to King Charles II (1630, r. 1660–85) for the Royal Touch. After a lapse of many years during the reign of his father, French King Louis XVI (1754, r. 1774–92) again touched thousands in the city of Rheims directly following his anointment. There was a strong popular demand for the king's special gift. Royalty everywhere was defined by divine approbation and was seen as tied to the superhuman.

The sacredness of kings was vested in objects and transferred through solemn ceremonies. Kings were created by spears, drums, animal skins, swords, mantles, sceptres, crowns, thrones, and jewels embodying royalty. Only by donning Charlemagne's age-old attire and insignia did the emperor-elect of the Holy Roman Empire acquire his supreme dignity. The Asante stool held the accumulated powers of ancestors: the stool transfigured the candidate into king; 'destooling' him took away kingship.

In prescribed series of solemn acts, officeholders and insignia changed aspirants into kings. Kings across the globe performed their roles in a calendar of celebrations fusing worldly rule and religious observation. This was never a sideshow: it stood at the heart of their power.

The sacred dimensions of kingship, broadcast in stone and script throughout history, have helped to convey an image of kings as almighty leaders, towering over their subjected peoples, living in magnificent palaces, and commanding an awesome machinery of power. After the French Revolution, these overblown images of royal propaganda were harnessed by antiroyalists, who used them to underline the arbitrariness, repression, and violence inherent in kingship. The past provides an endless repository of royal ineptitude, cruelty, and rapacity. Yet both royal propaganda and revolutionary fervour wildly overstated the power of kings and downplayed the limitations imposed by the divine mandate.

Pre-industrial royal power, lacking the advantages of modern technology, communications, and infrastructure, was a pitiful affair compared to that of modern leaders, democratic or authoritarian. Only in a small core area could royal authority be exerted effectively. Carrot-and-stick policies might help to maintain some coherence among more distant government agents, yet outlying areas were notoriously difficult to control. Inevitably all greater realms depended on layers of elites, who needed to be persuaded that compliance was in their best interests. Military force was used to subdue open rebellion, but repression was hazardous: escalation would erode the regime and invite rebels to step in and grab the throne. A widely shared and jointly enacted ideal of hierarchy, order, and divinely appointed sovereignty was the ubiquitous foundation of royal power. Elevated to unlikely heights, kings became the prisoners of their own lofty status. The façade of sacred and unassailable royal power hid frailty and discomfort.

Sages and warriors

What was expected from these kings? How did societies around the globe picture their ideal prince? And did these expectations ever materialize?

The connection with the sacred allowed kings to transcend common norms: ferocious and unconventional behaviour confirmed their special status. Incest, murder, and bloody sacrifice, often present in royal myths of origin, might still occur among latter-day dynastic founders and their successors. A potential for violent caprice forms part of the reputation of royals around the globe. However, the religious traditions so essential for rulership decreed a more moderate ideal of the king as guardian of harmony and order. Supremacy enabled kings to stand above parties, bring together conflicting interests, and, most importantly, to protect the weak. All world religions, in one way or another, underline these as the foremost functions of kings.

In East Asia and mainland South-East Asia, moral supremacy was accepted as the foundation of royal power. Buddhist kings were respected because they represented the accumulated merit of preceding generations; a virtuous life, for them, should be self-evident. The legendary Maurya Buddhist ruler Asoka (304, r. 268–232 BCE) converted to Buddhism and henceforth propagated the 'ten royal virtues': generosity, virtue, self-sacrifice, honesty, kindness, restraint, calmness, peacefulness, patience, and righteousness. Asoka's self-styled moral perfection was still invoked by the admirers of Thai King Bhumibol (1927, r. 1946–2016). Moving to Vietnam, China, Korea, and Japan, the mixture of Hindu and Buddhist ideals typical for mainland South-East Asia gave way to various amalgamations with Confucianism, Daoism, and Shintoism—yet the ideal of the king as moral exemplar prevailed here too. Supreme rule equalled moral perfection, permanent introspection, and self-improvement.

Sages ruled through example more than through action; providing for the poor and needy ranked high among the responsibilities assigned to them.

This ideal of the moral supremacy of the unmoving ruler, reiterated by Confucius and his followers, retained pre-eminence in the Chinese cultural sphere. Magistrates urged their sovereigns to give priority to learning, self-improvement, and the appropriate performance of rites (see Figure 3); outdoor excursions and military exploits needed to be kept to a minimum. The details of government and warfare were to be the remit of ministers and commanders. These exhortations exasperated energetic characters on the throne and led some of them to rebel against the restraints imposed on them. Others happily accepted their role as reclusive and passive symbols of power—mascots bringing to mind African sacred kings. In Japan the process was taken one step further: here the emperor's purity became wholly inviolable, while at the same time his political power was usurped by others, first by regents, later by imperial generals, the shoguns. Reigning and ruling were vested in two separate offices. Japanese dual kingship made visible a tension always present in royal power.

The standards of rulership in West Asia and Europe implied a more active style: first and foremost kings were lawgivers and judges. Babylonian king Hammurabi proudly stated: 'Let any wronged man who has a lawsuit come before ... me, the king of justice'. He explained his purpose elsewhere: 'to make justice prevail in the land, to abolish the wicked and the evil, to prevent the strong from oppressing the weak.' Echoes of these ringing statements can be found up until the demise of monarchy. Islamic rulers deferred to the holy statute of Islamic law and its scholars—the *Ulema*. Yet they cultivated their role as judges helping the needy and punishing wrongdoers among the mighty. Christian kings, too, accepted as their prime responsibility the mixture of justice, protection of the weak, and patronage of the church. The French King Louis IX (1214, r. 1226–79) famously

3. A loyal official remonstrating with the emperor (late 15th century, Ming China). Liu Jun, *c.*1475–1505 (Metropolitan Museum, New York).

received complainants under the oak in the woods of Vincennes. Louis XVI, fleeing revolutionary Paris in 1791, noted the loss of his right to grant pardon among his gravest concerns. Coronation oaths across Europe stipulated the protection of religion.

How could these sages, benefactors, and judges create harmony in an environment riven by warfare? Hammurabi's law code provides a suggestive answer: 'I annihilated enemies everywhere, I put an end to wars...I am indeed the shepherd who brings peace, whose scepter is just.' The successful warrior preceded the judge and the virtuous ruler: David came before Solomon; conquerors paved the way for Asoka. All dynastic founders ascended the throne as warriors before they could turn to lawmaking. In Europe and West and South Asia, the acclaimed deeds of dynastic predecessors invariably included acts of bravery. Valour was a requirement for kings, sultans, and shahs, groomed in a lifelong habit of hunting and outdoor exercises. Even docile and unadventurous figures could not ignore these expectations, and had themselves portrayed in heroic settings and in body armour. The macho stance of modern authoritarian leaders has a long pedigree.

The tasks of sages and warlords demand different qualities, perhaps best rendered as reactive and proactive. The key challenge was to create a balance between them, either through the king's personal prudence and moderation, or in the process of the sovereign's consultation with advisors. Kings were permanently pulled in different directions by incompatible requirements. Clemency invited weakness and could thus erode the sternness essential for royal justice. Generosity could lead to financial overextension and hence to the exploitation of subjects. Frugality would prevent such mishaps, yet no royal willingly embraced a reputation for stinginess. A late-medieval Burmese book of manners solved the problem by presenting its advice for kings in a series of clashing virtues: 'Gentleness causes oppression, severity creates enemies; these two things being known, one should take a medium course.' Gentleness and severity, we must assume, should be read as directed towards the mighty, who oppressed the population under indulgent kings, yet protested against the encroachments of strong kings. Implicitly, the maxim underlined that sovereigns needed to take into consideration the interests of different groups. Good kingship, more than anything else, was the capacity to navigate carefully between conflicting demands in permanently varying circumstances. Advice literature necessarily remained a mixed bag of examples and injunctions: no single coherent view of rulership could work for changing situations and a variety of characters on the throne.

In an 1857 letter Lord Acton stated that 'Power tends to corrupt, and absolute power corrupts absolutely. Great men are almost always bad men.' Three centuries earlier, the Florentine statesman Machiavelli had boldly expressed a similar view from a different perspective: only those willing to disregard Christian morality, he argued, can rule successfully. Acton and Machiavelli overstated their cases: kings were not necessarily always bad, neither did morality wholly preclude effective rule. Yet in past and present, political trafficking and top-level decision-making have been plagued by moral dilemmas. Kings, we can assume, took their religious mandate at least as seriously as modern politicians take the popular mandate. The fear of divine retribution must have been far more intimidating than the risk of an electoral thrashing. This has not prevented either category of powerholders from disregarding morality for the sake of political expediency. Few kings ever approached the ideals outlined for them: these were too demanding as well as inconsistent. Kings could retain an unblemished moral record only by leaving the hard choices in the hands of their ministers. If they wielded power themselves, their moral rectitude inevitably was compromised. Clashing expectations and insoluble dilemmas drove many rulers to escape into seclusion and passivity; an exasperating sense of personal inadequacy may have contributed to their brutalities.

A lifetime on the throne

Modern leaders rise to power at their physical and intellectual peak; they usually leave the scene before age manifestly undermines their performance. Elections can bring to power greybeards, but apparent incapacity to deal with the challenges of public office will undermine their chances of re-election. Only in authoritarian states do elderly leaders more often cling to power, either individually as revered dictators, or in a politburo-style collective gerontocracy. Leadership of elders occurs wherever power is concentrated in few hands, where terms of office remain open-ended, and succession is not determined by fixed procedures. Elders reticent to pass on leadership to the next generation are found with great frequency in manager-owned family businesses without a fixed retirement age. In the absence of such rules, it is difficult to willingly end an extended period in supreme office and pass on the reins to a successor. Voluntary abdication remains an exception in the history of kingship. This task did not end in early retirement softened with a golden handshake: it was to be performed until the last breath of the incumbent, and not only during office hours.

No modern state or company would consider appointing toddlers as executives, yet some kings reigned before they could walk or speak. Youngsters on the throne held an ambiguous position: they were educated by teachers who were at the same time subjected to their authority as kings. Disciplining the heir-apparent was a challenge for preceptors keen on securing a future for themselves and their dependants; teaching a minor king was even trickier. However, toddlers reigned under the tutelage of their elders, who exhorted them to respect their teachers. This was the standard opportunity for female power in history: mothers ruled as regents until their sons reached the age accepted as maturity, usually in their early teens. Until their sixth or seventh year, boys were surrounded mostly by women, who were responsible for the first stages of their education. Formal enthronement did not necessarily end the dependency of the king, although it almost inevitably led to greater tensions between the former regent and her son. Adolescents tested boundaries and challenged the authority of their elders; mothers were not always inclined to revert to their roles as passive observers—the combination was a recipe for political upheaval. Clashes were even more likely in the case of male regents, who themselves might have their eyes on the throne.

The sovereign's youth was a unique opportunity to create life-long bonds. Governors and governesses were the most trusted servants of boy kings, and often became their confidants and mentors. With wet nurses and youth companions, they formed a group set apart from the political tussle that perplexed most novice princes. The uncertainties of an adolescent ascending to supreme power and the presence of trusted servants make it easy to understand the frequent rise of favourites. However, political breakdown loomed if a single person stood between the sovereign and all others, controlling access to the prince, taking over policy deliberation, and distributing royal favours. The presence of a powerful favourite angered all who found themselves excluded. Upon the first signs of royal displeasure disgruntled advisors and courtiers would join in for the kill, chasing out the favourite and restoring their presence in the centre of power.

The collective biography of adolescent kings shows multiple examples of their liberation from the tutelage of mothers and favourites. After his first decade in power, Louis XIV of France dictated to his advisors a series of memoirs intended for the education of his son. These proud maxims celebrate the Sun King's personal rule in grand style—yet they implicitly show all the vexations of a youngster in power: dominance of a favourite, vested interests encroaching on royal power, the anxieties of public office for a child, and unending paperwork. Speaking to the Parisian supreme law court in 1648, the 9-year-old boy-king failed to remember his text and burst out in tears. Only with adulthood came confident sovereign power, at least for persons able to adequately perform this role. The changeover was not always easy. In 1665, Habsburg Emperor Leopold I, mourning the death of his former tutor, wrote to a friend that he could not share his grief with any of his courtiers, who would interpret his confidentiality as signalling the ascent of a new favourite. Nor was the entry into active political life always lasting. Upon the death in 1582 of his mentor and leading advisor, the Ming Wanli Emperor (1563, r. 1572–1620) started a period of effective rule. Frustrated by conflicts with his mother and with leading officials, he finally chose to withdraw into the palace. For all kings, governing engendered phases of disillusionment, manageable only in years of mental and physical resilience. These years of strength rarely covered more than two or perhaps three decades, whereas reigns could be much longer.

The birth of a successor was celebrated universally as a great occasion and prop for the dynasty. Doubts could surface during the adolescence of princes: rulers were reluctant to train their successors, fearing this would fuel impatience and rivalry. Once the heir reached adulthood, euphoria subsided and anxieties arose. Whether they liked it or not, heirs-apparent invariably attracted the disenfranchised as well as the ambitious, who hoped to see their status improve under the future ruler. Around the time a ruling king started noticing the diminution of his faculties, he also faced the challenge of a mature successor in the corridors of power, and a steady seepage of support among his advisors. The connection between father and son, king and successor, could easily turn sour. This process occurred everywhere, but it took different shapes.

Confucianism induced towering expectations on the side of the father and helped to create a sense of ineptitude and frustration on the son's part. In a drawn-out tragedy erupting in 1708, the Qing Kangxi Emperor (1654, r. 1661–1722) demoted and punished his preferred son and heir Yinreng, yet after agonizing doubts, restored the prince. Soon the process started anew: the ageing emperor noticed leading officials 'forming factions' around his son, and asked himself 'What is the meaning of this cleaving to the Heir-Apparent?' Finally in 1712 Yinreng was stripped of his rank and imprisoned. Kangxi later remarked that the clash had severely impaired his health—in fact it coincided with the onset of old age. An even darker story unfolded in neighbouring Korea, where King Yongjo (1694, r. 1724–76), after a series of increasingly violent clashes, finally forced his son Sado to commit suicide through suffocation in a rice chest. In her memoirs, the prince's widow vividly described the disheartening escalation of Yongjo's constant rebuke and Sado's increasingly desperate responses.

Father–son tensions in West and South Asia flared up when sons appeared as military leaders in their own right, while ageing fathers experienced difficulty in performing this essential role. Ottoman Sultan Süleyman (1494, r. 1520–66) worried about the popularity of his brawny son Mustafa at the very moment he became preoccupied with his fitness and appearance. Mustafa would not survive his father's anxieties. Safavid Shah Abbas (1557, r. 1586–1628), who had himself ascended the throne by ousting his father, noticed with dismay the rising reputation of his eldest son Safi among the soldiery, and had him executed in 1615. The many instances of father–son conflict in dynastic history demonstrate how the prospect of succession inflated to unhealthy proportions tensions present in most families.

Neither, however, did the absence of successors bode well for a comfortable old age. Candidates jockeyed for positions around the elderly king. The anticipation of an interregnum incited conflict around the king's deathbed. With or without impatient heirs, the end of long reigns coincided with the erosion of royal power. Ageing kings experienced a longer period of declining ambitions and capabilities. Leading his army during the 1566 campaign to Hungary, Süleyman had to be supported in his saddle by his servants: the sultan did not survive the exertions. Elderly kings gradually withdrew into a smaller circle of people and restricted themselves to a limited number of familiar activities. The shrinking of their horizons caused a situation akin to that of a boy-king: government was increasingly taken over by others. Confidants shielded the decrepit sovereign and took power into their own hands. Few long-reigning kings escaped from dependency in youth as well as in old age.

Tricks of the trade

Superior rank made it difficult to approach kings. The obligations attached to the position intimidated many incumbents, and froze some of them into immobility. For these lone figures, affection and trust were always tinged with danger. Siblings and children, stakeholders in the dynastic venture, could easily turn into rivals. Spouses and concubines might prefer their son over their partner, particularly in polygynous settings. Unreserved friendship with advisors entailed the risk of dependency and would give rise to discontent among courtiers. Even the suspicion of the rise of a favourite might undermine royal power.

Manuals for kingship rehearsed royal virtues, idealizing paragons on the throne, and pointing to the mishaps caused by bad kings. These tracts were written by clerics and magistrates eager to train their royal pupils to become just rulers. Alternatively, they used the moral code as an instrument to curb the awesome powers of a prince run wild. Some of these advisors mixed their exhortations with practical advice; others went further and produced manuals for political survival. Machiavelli's *Prince* is the most famous and provocative of such tracts. Many kings left instructions for their successors; some produced lengthy memoirs or diaries. These texts comprise bland assertions of royal grandeur, practical guidelines, and, incidentally, more probing examinations. Yet they all reflect the ideals imposed on royals as well as the daily tribulations of kingship.

Unsurprisingly, fathers told their sons to limit indulgence in sex and alcohol, warning them that overexcitation will ruin health, composure, and authority—typically, they had not heeded these warnings in their own lives. Instructions point to the need for a steady rhythm of the day, week, and year, creating a balance between toil and relaxation. They invariably stress the towering importance of religious observance, paperwork, consultation with ministers, audiences, and the administration of justice. Warnings followed never to disregard requests and petitions: unresponsive kings generate discontented populations. Physical exertions and learning were weighed differently in various dynastic traditions.

Kings reminded their sons of the need to respond to their subjects' concerns and counselled them about deliberations with ministers. How were they expected to behave during such encounters? Princes were told to adopt dignified deportment and dress, yet one injunction was particularly emphasized: reticence in speaking. The Chinese Tang Taizong emperor (598, r. 626–49) explained why: 'If an ordinary man says something wrong, it could bring shame on him. If the ruler has a slip of the tongue, the consequences could be disastrous.' Many texts repeat the idea that chattering kings undermined their dignity and eroded their power. Kaikavus, an 11th-century Persian princeling and the last of his house to rule, stated in the book of advice he wrote for his son that 'silence is double security and loquacity double folly'. In his remarkably candid diary, a 17th-century Frisian stadholder in the Dutch Republic cautioned himself: 'don't cause trouble with my tongue; even if I know better, I should stop myself from speaking out'. A few decades later, Louis XIV of France told his son that 'speaking a lot is a most dangerous habit for the prince to develop'.

Royalty drew large numbers of supplicants: having the king's ear brought chances for justice, benefits, and advancement. Royals found themselves at the heart of a maelstrom of requests. Most rulers knew that the rewards and punishments they meted out formed the backbone of their personal power. Kings could never control all benefactions or review all penalties; yet they understood that at least the most important of these decisions should remain in their hands. Han Feizi, a 3rd-century-BCE Chinese sage, described rewards and punishments as the emperor's 'claws and teeth' and warned against leaving them in the hands of ministers. However, the throng of petitioners necessitated drastic reticence in speech. Habsburg Emperor Charles V warned his son that promises made on the spur of the moment returned with a vengeance. It is no coincidence that we often read about kings expressing themselves in the vaguest of terms: 'Justice shall be done', or 'We shall see'.

The advantages of silence were equally obvious in consultations with advisors. Kings should listen to the advice of their ministers before speaking themselves. Indeed, they could best adopt an attitude of inscrutable detachment. Only in this way would ministers be invited to speak their minds rather than repeat what they surmised the king wanted to hear. The advice of Han Feizi neatly captures this idea: 'be silent as though in a drunken stupor.... be thicker, be clumsier than ever! Let others say their piece...gain knowledge thereby.' The English statesman and writer Francis Bacon (1561–1626) likewise stressed that the king should hide his preferences, otherwise ministers would simply agree and 'sing him a song of "Placebo"'. Observing the ministers in dignified silence made it easier to distinguish between good advice and self-serving recommendations.

Effective rule required the presence of a talented team of advisors. Rulers, therefore, needed to be able to recognize and reward talent. Tang Taizong stated that a good ruler 'employs men as a skilled carpenter selects wood...straight or crooked, long or short, each piece is useful'. Assigning to each talent the most suitable task was a key quality for kings. Luck and intuition, Louis XIV intimated in his memoirs, were part of this story, yet there were rules—and they, too, are repeated in a great diversity of texts. No minister should ever dominate government to such an extent that he could be perceived as usurping royal power. An accumulation of honours and powers on the shoulders of a single person should be prevented: the highest-ranking among the elites—royal princes, leading nobles—could not be allowed to claim as their right a share in government. This would create rivals rather than servants.

For all kings, and more generally for all executives, it was important to find a balance between personal supervision and delegation, control and trust. Having multiple ministers who could mutually exert some control made this easier. Famously, Louis XIV stated in his memoirs that 'the jealousy of one checked the ambitions of the other'. A group of advisors should be big enough to generate different perspectives and positions, but not so unwieldy that it could no longer effectively convene as one body. Joint sessions were not sufficient to discuss the portfolios of ministers in great depth: this could be done only in individual work sessions with the king. Often, kings preferred to study proposals and decrees in solitude, writing their comments and corrections in the margins, undisturbed by the presence of ministers. Many preferences and customs can be found in royal memoirs and instructions, but no single ideal would persist in all circumstances. It was always easier to make clear the absolute don'ts of government than to propose a list of unequivocal guidelines.

Chapter 3
Women and dynastic power

Queens regnant

Dynasties took shape in very different ways, yet they all viewed government first and foremost as a male prerogative. Only rarely did women preside over the council and lead armies into war. No lasting examples of matriarchy can be found in the annals of dynastic history, but queens did rule. These queens-regnant were weighed down not only by the substantial burdens of kingship: they were wedged in by the tensions between their gender role and the requirements of power holding.

Religious creeds and learned traditions universally warned against female assaults on the male-held privilege of sovereignty. Notwithstanding this preference for men and their overwhelming predominance in king lists, a careful reading of sources uncovers myriads of active queen-mothers and queen-consorts who shared power with kings. Whenever these women failed to shroud their activities in piety and compliance, they risked defamation. Chroniclers were disposed to equate female power with wiliness and cruelty, the warped counterimages of male acumen and strength. Much has been done recently to salvage women in power from oblivion and vilification. As a consequence, it is now possible to outline the variety of roles women played in the dynastic setting, taking into account the limitations imposed on them as well as their opportunities to wield power.

Almost invariably, queens-regnant came to the fore during succession struggles. In the absence of male candidates, women were the sole option to secure the continuation of the ruling house. Faced with the threat of extinction, patrilineal dynasties could push forward their women as legitimate successors. Examples of earlier ruling queens facilitated the rise of women to the throne, but military force was often necessary to subdue unconvinced male contestants. With the ascendancy of the deceased king's sister or daughter, royal blood overruled gender bias.

Male succession violence abounds in history, and it often came close to destroying chances for dynastic survival. The Sasanian-Persian Empire (224–651) witnessed two brief consecutive reigns of women in 630–1. Typically, a series of bloody clashes among male contenders brought two sisters to the throne. After losing a war with the Byzantines, their father, Khosrow II (570, r. 590–628), was deposed by one of his sons. The Baghdad scholar Al-Tabari relates how the latter, enthroned as Kavad II, was pushed by the elites to have his deposed father killed and 'wept copiously' after the deed had been done. Notwithstanding his alleged grief, the new king subsequently ordered the execution of almost all potential male heirs, 'seventeen of his brothers, men of good education, bravery, and the manly virtues'. Kavad's own speedy death, from the plague ravaging Persia in the same year, initiated a series of short reigns, first by his minor son, then by a usurping general, and finally by his half-sister Borandokht, followed by another half-sister, Azarmidokht.

Endless other examples essentially replicate the Sasanian story. A Chinese chronicler reports that, when in 1616 the Sultan of Patani in South-East Asia died without a son, 'his relatives all fought for the throne ... until there was none ... left. Thus, they enthroned a female chief as queen.' Succession crises could be caused simply by the lack of male progeny, yet they were most often exacerbated by violence. The absence of an heir of indisputable legitimacy triggered violent competition among eligible males; military defeat and the loss of prestige of the incumbent ruler created opportunities for usurpers. In such cases, the rule of women was accepted grudgingly as the last remaining option to prevent dynastic extinction and usurpation by outsiders.

Queens-regnant almost inevitably started from a weak position: they were tolerated in their position by elites who preferred a female representative of the old ruling house to the ascendancy of a usurper from among their own ranks. Queens emerging in such circumstances needed to generate support, by appeasing the mighty and promising just government to their peoples. Everywhere, women on the throne invested considerable energies to overcome hesitations among their servants and subjects. Borandokht promised her people to restore justice, rebuild bridges, and grant tax remits. On her newly minted gold coins (see Figure 4) she proudly stated: 'Buran, restorer of the Race of Gods'. Not everybody was equally impressed. A chronicler reporting on Borandokht's short reign cites the Prophet Muhammad, who allegedly commented on her rise to power by stating that 'Never will succeed such a nation as makes a woman their ruler'.

The dearth of male princes, which gave rise to female succession in the first place, could lead to a string of women on the throne. The remarkable concentration of queens in 16th-century England and 18th-century Russia was the consequence of a persisting succession crisis and by no means indicated a preference for women rulers. Other examples are less straightforward. In the 17th century, an unbroken line of women governed in the sultanates of Patani as well as Aceh—located in modern Thailand and Indonesia, respectively. Elite kingmakers and the ruling

4. Sasanian gold dinar (630–1) with Borandokht's image.

sultana consistently designated female relatives. The record of
Patani and Aceh suggests that the reign of a first queen could
forge a path for female successors and reduce the prejudice
against women on the throne.

Once a woman had effectively ruled for decades, the likelihood of
female succession increased. Clusters of female power strike the
eye in world history. Between 750 and 675 BCE five queens in a
row ruled the Kedarite Arab tribal federation (in the area of
current South-Eastern Syria and North-East Jordan). Kingdoms
south of Egypt left a legacy of reigning queens. Between 284 BCE
and 314 CE, the Kingdom of Kush counted a remarkable number
of queens-regnant. The New Testament refers to the 'candace'
or queen of Ethiopia; in his *Ecclesiastical History*, Eusebius
(*c.*260–340) glossed that the country was still ruled by women
following 'ancestral custom' in his days. During the reign of
Wu Zetian (624, r. 690–705), the only empress who ever formally
ruled the Chinese Empire, several queens and empresses sat on

the throne in Korea and Japan. African history is particularly rich in examples of ruling women. Queen Nzinga of Ndongo-Matamba (current Angola) fought her way to power and throughout her reign struggled to be accepted as sovereign, yet she opened an era where queens became the rule. The 19th-century Merina kingdom of Madagascar was ruled most of the time by queens. Between 1800 and 2005, six 'rain-queens' reigned in South African Lovedu, a unique example of unbroken female succession, where males were never even considered.

The ascendancy of women did not necessarily safeguard dynastic continuity: female rulership complicated marriage and childbirth. The Lovedu rain-queens were pictured as males and received daughters from village chiefs in their harem. Male lovers needed to remain invisible, their existence a carefully kept secret. Disregarding these precautions and openly showing her lover, the last rain-queen ruled only briefly before she was hit by a lethal unexplained disease. Rumours suggested that her unconventional behaviour may have led to poisoning. Overall, sovereign rule was seen as quintessentially male and therefore incompatible with female fertility and motherhood: women in power jeopardized their powers of procreation. In practice the combined demands of motherhood and government must often have been daunting. Between 1737 and 1756 Maria Theresa (1717, r. 1740–80) bore sixteen children while steering Austria through a phase of grave military and political challenges.

Marriage was not without risk for queens-regnant. The appearance of a husband of high noble or foreign princely extraction raised the spectre of usurpation: males fitted uncomfortably in the passive role commonly ascribed to female consorts. This was one of the arguments used in defence of the 'Salic law' preventing women from ascending the throne in France and the Holy Roman Empire: foreign male spouses were expected to usurp power, secretly or openly. The story of the first English queen-regnant, Mary I Tudor (1516, r. 1553–8), became a cautionary tale for Protestants. In 1554, she married the Catholic Habsburg heir-apparent, who would soon rule Spain as Philip II. In the following years Mary earned the epithet 'bloody' by forcefully attempting to restore Catholicism in England. Neither queens nor the elites in their environment were necessarily eager to welcome powerful foreign male consorts. In this sense, the attitude of Elizabeth I of England (1533, r. 1558–1603), the 'virgin queen' who considered many husbands but never married, reflected common concerns.

Conversely, if queens remained unwedded and childless, their demise risked bringing an end to the ruling house. Indeed, the rule of women frequently coincided with dynastic change. In the three millennia between Merneith (c.2950 BCE) and Cleopatra VII (69, r. 51–30 BCE), eight Egyptian queens appear to have reigned in their own right (see Figure 5); at least three among them, including Cleopatra, ruled as the last surviving representatives of their dynastic line. The forty-year reign of Gudit (937–78) in Ethiopia, shrouded in myth but documented in several sources, bridged the changeover from the Axum Empire (c.100–938) to the Zagwe dynasty (c.978–1270). The death of Queen Arwa of Yemen (1048, r. 1101–38) spelled the end of the short-lived Sulayhid dynasty. After the death of Habsburg Emperor Charles VI, Maria Theresa was crowned in two kingdoms, but she could not formally rule as emperor, a dignity expressly reserved for men. Only through her husband Francis Stephen of Lorraine could the elective dignity be regained and transmitted to Joseph II. Continuity in power was arranged by co-rulership and the relabelling of the dynasty as the House of Habsburg-Lorraine.

Just, merciful, and valiant queens figure in chronicles and myths, yet forceful women on the throne often inspired vehement criticism among scholars as well as in the wider public. Confucian literati evoked the memory of Wu Zetian to show that government in the hands of a woman would inevitably wreak havoc. The empress

5. Egyptian Queen Hatshepsut, icon of female power. Head from an Osiride statue of Hatshepsut, 1479–1458 BCE (Metropolitan Museum, New York).

still haunts popular stories as a lascivious and violent 'fox spirit', undermining moral order by transgressing gender norms. Likewise, after more than a millennium, Ethiopian peasants today recount the violent misdeeds of legendary Queen Gudit. Vigorous women, apparently, were more likely to be remembered as evil characters than their equally formidable male fellow-rulers.

Was it easier for women to obtain paramount power in some regions? The bias against the regiment of women was strongest where it coincided with patrilineal succession. In imperial China the dominance of the male line was manifest in social life as well as in government. China's extensive administrative machinery, dominated by gentlemen-scholars, further distanced women from power. The Steppe conquest dynasties ruling China, notably the Mongol Yuan (1279–1368) and the Manchu Qing (1644–1912), left more leeway to women in daily life, yet these dynasties did not bring women closer to power. An overriding patrilineal tradition and a successful prohibition against ruling women can also be found in the Ottoman Empire. Reproduction through slave concubines of indifferent background underlined the pre-eminence of the patriline here, and no woman ever ruled in her own right.

The patriline dominated in Central Asia, the pre-Columbian Americas, and Europe, but the female lineage still made a difference here. Safavid and Mughal princes married princesses of noble lineage, and high-ranking women from the dynasty were a notable presence in these domains, even if they failed to reach the throne. Noble ancestry was a requirement for Mongol spouses, who wielded power only in the name of their husbands or minor sons. Aztec queens connected the ruling kings to a prestigious earlier dynasty through their Toltec genealogy; Inca queens were either the king's sisters, or women from powerful noble lineages. The characteristically European combination of dynastic intermarriage and monogamy made male and female pedigree almost equally relevant. Nevertheless, there was great variety: women ruled in Spain, England, Scandinavia, and Russia, but were barred from succession in France and in the Holy Roman Empire. Striking and persistent examples of women holding sovereign power can be found in smaller polities of Africa and Austronesia, regions also known for examples of matrilineal succession.

The main religious creeds were hesitant at best about female power. Religious authorities thundered against women in power everywhere. With his 1558 diatribe, *The First Blast of the Trumpet Against the Monstrous Regiment of Women*, the Scottish Calvinist John Knox advocated the widely held view that women on the throne were unnatural. His intervention was determined first and foremost by Mary Tudor's actions against Protestantism. Elsewhere, too, religion was sometimes invoked to criticize, prevent, or end female rule. In 1699, the reign of the fourth Sultana of Aceh ended in tumult when a religious decree against the rule of women arrived, allegedly issued in Mecca. However, elite support for the sultanas waned in the same years, and religious authority may simply have offered a convenient additional argument. Moral and religious traditions always offered a repository of arguments against women on the throne. The leading protagonists in succession crises could disregard such objections; alternatively, they might use them to revert to the standard of male power.

Queen-mothers and reign mates

Kings in most parts of the world were expected to lead armies into battle and show physical prowess, traits associated with masculinity. How could women cope with the strong associations between masculine behaviour and supreme power? Women-warriors, abounding in mythology and literature, can also be found in the historical record. Female palace guards protected the Leopard Kings of Dahomey as well as kings and sultans in South-East Asia. Queens themselves could act as fierce amazons. The Greek geographer Strabo (64 BCE–24 CE) reported the military actions of the Candace of Kush, 'a masculine sort of woman and blind in one eye'. Gudit of Ethiopia, another warrior-queen, allegedly had only one breast. Seventeenth-century Queen Nzinga of Ndongo-Matamba commanded armies, smoked a pipe, and assembled concubines. Ruling queens could lead armies into battle, wear male attire—and might, like Nzinga, eventually choose to redefine themselves as male.

The image of ferocious women-warriors defined female power as legendary and out of bounds; these queens performing as males confirmed the common association between masculinity and leadership. These same gendered views, however, made it relatively easy to accept the mother of an infant-king as regent. Queen-mothers ruled by upholding the sovereignty of the male heir. Widowhood liberated them from the constrictions placed on the queen-consort, who was expected to remain in the shadow of her governing husband. Protecting their sons' lawful inheritance, widows could combine active rulership with the characteristics attributed to good women: chastity, modesty, and mercifulness. This role was accepted with less difficulty than the queen-regnant's unmitigated mixture of power and femininity.

The presence of an heir made a key difference, even before the birth of the child. Hindu dowager-queens, expected to undergo the traditional *sati* ritual of widow-burning upon the death of their ruling husband, used their pregnancy as an argument to escape from the rite, survive, and rule in the name of the royal child. Some apparently even feigned pregnancies and later resorted to adoption to conserve their position. The presence of a junior male heir defined the regency as a temporary exception; mothers would stage their government as preparing the ground for the king-to-be. Their role was to maintain union and peace during the interregnum, assisted by male commanders and ministers.

The very fact that women could not rule in their own names made them more suitable as regents than male relatives, who themselves might endeavour to seize the throne. Mothers and ministers helped to counterbalance princes of the blood in regency councils. France, the Ottoman Empire, and China, three realms known for patrilineal descent and prohibitive attitudes towards the rule of women, are famous for their powerful dowagers. After the death of Henry II in 1559, Catherine de Medici (1515–89) became a leading figure during the reigns of her sons Francis II, Charles IX, and, to a lesser extent, Henry III. Her two 17th-century successors, Marie de Medici and Anne of Austria, fulfilled the same role, though they never quite matched their predecessor's record. The striking career of Kösem Sultan (1589–1651) trumps even that of Catherine de Medici. Starting out as the favourite concubine of Ahmed I, she acted as dowager empress (*valide sultan*) for three consecutive sultans: her sons Murad IV and Ibrahim I, and her grandson Mehmed IV. Eventually she was executed in a coup orchestrated by Mehmed's mother Hadice Turhan, who became the next *valide sultan*. In France and the Ottoman Empire, mothers were notably present in the later 16th and early 17th centuries. Chinese history includes several powerful dowagers, but the last striking instance stands isolated. Qing Dowager Empress Cixi (1835–1908) held *de facto* power as regent from 1861 to her death, first ruling in the name of her son the Tongzhi emperor, later for her nephew cum adopted son, the Guanxu emperor.

Conflict threatened when minors reached maturity and wanted to take the reins of power into their own hands. Would their powerful mothers placidly retreat into the shadowy corridors of informal power? In 1632, Kösem had accepted the ascent of her energetic son Murad IV; yet in 1648 she refused to step aside for Hadice Turhan, mother of the new boy-sultan Mehmed IV. In 1889, Cixi had to endure the co-rule of her maternal nephew and adopted son, but after a decade regained her supremacy. Marie de Medici clashed with her son Louis XIII, had to flee France, and died in exile in 1642. Other mothers never even allowed their sons to govern. After the death of her husband emperor Bakaffa (d. 1730) dowager-empress Mentewab of Ethiopia (1706–73) ruled in the name of her boy-son until the latter's death in 1755, incarcerated his spouse, and continued ruling for her infant grandson until 1769. While she was the dominant power for almost forty years, she never took the step to openly proclaim sovereign rule.

Others who started out as queen-mothers had no qualms about eliminating their wards and formally ascending to the throne. Nzinga ruled in the name of her deceased brother's son, but soon got rid of the boy. Wu Zetian was a concubine and a dowager-empress before she stepped forward as empress—and she made sure to first eradicate her most likely rivals. Russian empress Elisabeth pushed aside the boy-Tsar Ivan VI to secure her power; her designated successor Peter III ruled only a few months before he was outflanked by his spouse Catharina. Peter's deposition and death made possible the reign of this robust tsaritsa.

For many queens in history we cannot determine with certainty whether or not they ruled in the name of their sons. The impressive list of candaces ruling Kush, for instance, may well include several queen-mothers. The presence of a boy-king did not necessarily reduce the woman ruling in his name: queen-mothers could be as powerful as queens-regnant. However, a minor but nominally sovereign male heir made unnecessary the ultimate step of granting full regal powers to a woman. Widowed mothers were the most common and most accepted women in power. As we shall see in the final chapter of this book, there is an echo of this in the contemporary world: a surprising number of modern women 'inherited' leadership, following the violent deaths of their governing fathers or husbands.

African history shows multiple queen-mothers quite similar to those in Europe and Asia—Mentewab is a striking example. Yet there was another, very different category of queen-mothers here as well. These women ruled side-by-side with mature kings, as permanent female complements rather than as temporary stand-ins for boy-kings. Such female 'reign mates' were never the king's spouse, and rarely his biological mother. In the matrilineal

Asante federation, the queen-mother (*asanthemaa*) and king (*asantehene*) shared membership of the royal lineage. Kings and their female reign mates held complementary responsibilities, and each played a role in determining the succession of the other. Male–female complementarity recurred at all political levels of the Asante federation. Another example of dual rule can be found in nearby patrilineal Dahomey, where the queen-mother (*kpojito*) was usually a palace woman, a generation above the king, but not his biological mother. She ranked among the kingmakers of the realm, but did not belong to the royal lineage. On the contrary, this queen-mother represented the non-royal, the conquered, the commoners, and the women—in everything the king's opposite, yet his indispensable counterpart. Finally, the *Iyoba* of Benin in West Africa underlines the variety: this was in fact the king's biological mother, a palace woman who had given birth to the king (*oba*). On the whole, African queen-mothers were a lasting presence rather than a temporary solution for a minor king.

The notion of complementarity of male and female power, as the two necessary components of a balanced realm, can be recognized in many places, from Africa to the Inca domains. Whether or not these women were the ruling king's mother, they were often seen as mothers of their peoples. This type of leadership did not necessarily clash with the qualities ascribed to women.

Spouses, concubines, and mistresses

Queens-regnant held full royal powers; queen-mothers often lacked only the final accolade of formal sovereignty. In contrast to these acclaimed power holders, wives and concubines were expected to remain in the shadow of the male sovereign. Religion, charity, and patronage of the arts were within their purview, and they shared the responsibility for arranging family alliances. Exemplary morality might justify their stepping forward as intermediaries, pleading for their peoples. Several queens-consort in history have been presented as merciful complements to the stern justice of the male sovereign. Zubaida, wife of the Abbasid Caliph Harun al-Rashid (766, r. 783–809), was widely remembered for the wells and fountains she set up for pilgrims. Her accomplishments were appreciated as perfecting those of her reigning husband. Conspicuous political activity, however, commonly met with disapproval because it suggested the weakness of the male sovereign. How could a man unable to command the dependants in his household ever manage to rule his domains?

Outside of their limited circle of accepted activities, spouses could hold power indirectly and informally, through their ruling companion. This grey area remains largely unfathomable. Women could play their roles as supportive and devout wives with relish, while effectively managing the affairs of the realm. Conversely, the classic attitude of meekness could come naturally to spouses who were entirely isolated from political decision-making. Neither the silences in chronicles nor the negative clichés about meddling women tell us much about the actual political agency of spouses.

Monogamy and polygyny created different positions, and there was considerable variety in each. While almost all kings practised polygyny, the status of their consorts differed. The Abbasid Caliphs in Baghdad after the death of Harun al-Rashid and most Ottoman Sultans after the conquest of Constantinople (1453) discontinued the practice of royal marriage and had only concubines. The hierarchies among these ladies were determined by the affections of the prince: his preferred partners were ranked above their competitors. Alternatively, a ranking existed where several women—not necessarily limited to the four wives accepted by Islam—held married status, whereas a more numerous group served as concubines. This was customary in Safavid Iran and Mughal India. Finally, a single queen or empress could preside over a hierarchy of lesser ladies—the form common in China.

The presence of multiple women in the harem was not tainted by associations with immorality, yet ageing favourites might resent the rise of young and attractive rivals. At any point, the rise of a youthful concubine might overturn established hierarchies. The birth of a son could promote her overnight to the status of potential queen-mother. This form of advancement was common in the Ottoman Empire, where concubines after giving birth to a son were no longer sexually available for the sultan: the presence of a son and potential successor now defined the mother's responsibilities. Chinese empresses were not necessarily threatened by the pregnancies of concubines: they could legally claim the children and appropriate the benefits of motherhood. A ruling son, however, might later promote his biological mother to higher status.

In late medieval and early modern Europe, monogamous marriage necessarily entailed the presence of one woman as queen or empress, with a high birth rank and a conspicuous role in the ceremonies of the court. Herself a scion of a ruling house, she was expected to maintain contacts with her relatives and support family interests in the European dynastic web. This expanded her sphere of activities, but also raised a thorny question: did she represent the interests of her own patriline, or those of her acquired family? Marriages concluded to celebrate peace treaties brought home queens associated with the arch enemy. These young women arrived from distant places, cultivated outlandish habits, and spoke foreign languages. Their retinues competed for offices and honours with the locals. Xenophobia and animosity were easily roused. Marie-Antoinette was welcomed in France as *l'autrichienne* before she was criticized for her initial failure to produce children and her indulgence in excesses. Her death on the scaffold during the Revolution remained an exception, yet a disapproving attitude awaited many foreign queens. Childbirth changed the balance: not only did it secure dynastic continuity, it also ensured the loyalty of the mother, now tied to the interests of her offspring more than to those of her lineage.

Monogamy restricted succession to legitimate offspring, but did not prevent rulers from seeking sexual adventures. Many queens witnessed the rise of female rivals, young and attractive women who, either on their own or with the assistance of ambitious courtiers, managed to enthral the king. Womanizers on the throne, conversely, used their position to secure a constant flow of attractive ladies, mostly from among palace women. Some affairs lasted longer and gave more opportunities to the mistress. The most successful among these women rose to become shadow queens, tainted by the illicit nature of their position but far more powerful than royal wives. Louis XIV's queen Marie-Thérèse, the daughter of Philip IV of Spain and the richest prize of Europe, needed to accept her husband's infatuations, including the conspicuously visible presence of mistresses such as Madame de Montespan. The king sedately counselled his son never to let his heart interfere with matters of state, yet he did not himself abide by this recommendation. From Louis XIV's youth to his deathbed, women were a powerful presence—though not primarily his queen and mother of the heir-apparent.

European mistresses could momentarily approach, match, or even eclipse the power of a favourite minister. Nevertheless, their status remained vulnerable: counterforces could capitalize on fears of divine retribution, or alternatively provide eye-catching rivals for the king's attention. Only in exceptional cases were mistresses able to prolong their status beyond the period of sexual infatuation. Former sweethearts could become confidantes and might serve as procuresses for royal pleasures. Others mimicked the role of the queen-mother by becoming the champions of their children, of royal blood but lacking eligibility for the throne. In 1683, shortly after the death of his queen Marie-Thérèse, Louis XIV secretly married the former governess of his illegitimate children, Madame de Maintenon. This pious surrogate mother of Madame de Montespan's children was the dominant female presence at the French court in the final decades of the Sun King's rule—and she experienced a moment of glory when two bastard princes were temporarily accepted as legitimate heirs to the throne. However, not even Madame de Maintenon could reap the ultimate reward: the established and lasting position of queen-mother.

Systems, lifecycles, roles

Women found their way to power in dynasties across the globe, notwithstanding the pervasive criticism of moral-religious codes. Where patrilineal succession was at its strictest, they rose to power mostly as queen-mothers. Queens-regnant, always the exception, were accepted somewhat more easily in regions where female lineage was seen as significant. Childless spouses were vulnerable everywhere, although the Chinese empress could profit from the fertility of concubines. Only in the case of the queen-regnant could childbirth complicate rather than consolidate female power, because her child might blur the distinction between sovereign rule and regency. Sexual attraction catapulted women to brief supremacy everywhere, yet as widows and mothers they enjoyed more lasting and stable positions.

In most cases the power of women was related to the absence or temporary weakness of male powerholders. Succession struggles, boy-kings, and weakened greybeards opened doors for daughters, mothers, spouses, and favourites. Interlacing dynastic lifecycles created opportunities for women to step forward when their male counterparts were absent or unable to hold the reins of power. Only where the complementarity of male and female power was established did ruling women form a lasting and necessary component of the political order. Here female reign mates co-existed permanently with mature and active male rulers. This was the case in parts of Africa and perhaps to some extent in

Austronesia. To be sure, many wives elsewhere assisted their husbands with the burdens of government or even acted as *de facto* rulers, yet their influence can be gauged with some precision only in rare cases.

Women could maximize their power by judiciously conforming to gender expectations. Madame de Maintenon publicly deployed activities mostly in fields traditionally associated with women: religious patronage and the education of girls. When the council met in her presence, she sat in an alcove, concentrating on her needlework. Only by reading the memoirs of courtiers and the

6. African Queen Nzinga with bow, leading warriors. Sketch by Antonio Cavazzi, printed in Ezio Bassani, ed., *Un Cappuccino nell'Africa nera del seicento: I disegni dei Manoscritti Araldi del Padre Giovanni Antonio Cavazzi da Montecuccolo* (Milan 1987).

international correspondence of diplomats and sovereigns who appreciated her influence, do we fully understand the powers of the Sun King's spouse. In 1730, Queen-Mother Mentewab of Ethiopia, the undisputed leader for decades, had herself depicted as the loyal mother of her 7-year-old son, crowned with the paraphernalia of sovereign power. After Wu Zetian, Chinese dowagers could accept power only in disavowal of their predecessor's usurpation. When Tang dowager-empress Guo (d. 848) was asked to rule in the name of her son, she allegedly exclaimed in distress: 'are you saying that I should become another Empress Wu?...Since ancient times, when has a woman ever ruled the world and established order...?'

The example of Nzinga reminds us of the opposite strategy: confronting gendered expectations by adopting male manners (see Figure 6). Warrior-queens unfolded the full panoply of gendered kingship, up to the point where their identity shifted from female to male. The spectacular careers of such women left their imprint on history and mythology, where they could be transformed into untarnished heroines or depraved she-devils. Their exploits ranged so far beyond the ordinary that they confirmed traditional standards. Variants of these two strategies and the responses they typically generated among the wider public can be traced into the 21st century.

Chapter 4
Embedding the family

Establishing genealogies

Childless upstart kings appear in the historical record as insignificant interludes at best. Yet even successful usurpers who were succeeded by their relatives did not always manage to establish an enduring ruling house. Newcomers needed to prove to themselves as well as to others that their house was worthy to carry the mantle of kingship. In different proportions, royal descent, martial valour, and moral rectitude formed part of the recipe. Moreover, rulers sought confirmation by cultivating links to earlier dynastic legacies and by seeking the approbation of religious authorities.

While supreme power as a rule required imposing ancestry, not all founders of dynasties could boast royal or even noble pedigree. The first emperors of the Han (206 BCE–220 CE) and the Ming (1368–1644) dynasties both came from peasant backgrounds and fought their way to the throne. Everywhere, striking military success could compensate for an indifferent background because it suggested personal valour as well as divine favour. Nevertheless, pedigree was an important component of royal legitimacy in most places: it is rare to find kings who openly admitted their modest provenance and did not make any effort to establish a more dignified genealogy.

Elaborate family trees were produced to buttress royal dignity. The genealogies and king lists of ruling houses covered up demographic mishaps and confounded actual kinship relations with coveted affinities: the lineage was adjusted and embellished. Family trees placed the prince in a hierarchically ordered view of the world and of history. Establishing a relationship with distant and sometimes wholly imaginary forebears meant appropriating a share of their towering prestige.

Legendary conquerors loom large in history. The myths of Alexander the Great and Chinggis Khan (see Figure 7) resounded in the decades and centuries following their demise. Echoes of Alexander's endeavours reached all corners of Eurasia. His image was invoked far beyond the successor empires of Ptolemaic Egypt, Seleucid Asia, and Antigonid Macedonia. Other conquerors likewise served as examples for their epigones. Timur (1336, r. 1370–1405) cultivated Chinggis Khan by accommodating one of the conqueror's male descendants as 'puppet-khan' at his court and by marrying a Chinggisid princess: he could now pose as a son-in-law of his great example. In their turn, the Mughals of India prided themselves on their double descent from Timur through the male line and Chinggis Khan through the female line. Their genealogy fused with the myths of two conquerors.

Muhammad (570–632) has been revered first and foremost as a prophet; yet his religious mission coincided with military success, and it would obtain dynastic form. Muhammad left no sons, neither was next-of-kin succession practised by the first four caliphs, who were selected by the community of believers. These 'rightly guided caliphs', however, were all related to the Prophet through marriage. Only gradually did the caliphate become hereditary, and this process coincided with a succession struggle that soon acquired doctrinal overtones. The murder of the third Caliph Uthman (579, r. 644–56), member of the leading Umayya family, initiated a phase of internecine strife. His successor Ali faced serious disturbances and was likewise killed. Another

7. The epitome of dynastic conquest: Chinggis Khan entering Beijing. Siege of Beijing (1213–14), Jami' al-tawarikh, Rashid al-Din (Bibliothèque nationale de France. Département des Manuscrits. Division orientale. Supplément persan 1113, fol. 65v).

powerful member of the Umayya family, Muawiyah I
(602, r. 661–80), used the occasion to establish himself in power
as caliph. With his coup, he founded the hereditary line of
Umayyad Caliphs (661–750). However, hereditary succession was
against the rules of early Islam and further provoked the
disgruntled followers of Ali. In the ensuing conflicts, Ali's sons
Hasan and Husayn, grandsons of the Prophet through his
daughter Fatima, lost their lives. They became martyrs for the
'party of Ali' soon known as *Shi'a*, which gradually diverged from
the *Sunni* adherents of the caliphs by developing different
doctrines and styles of devotion.

Muhammad, Ali, the Umayyads, and the next caliphal dynasty,
the Abbasids, shared a common ancestor. Belonging to this 'house
of the Prophet' became a status marker of myriads of Islamic
powerholders. Elites across the Islamic world still claim descent
from the Prophet's house, as do the current rulers of Morocco,
Jordan, and Brunei. The Prophet's charisma stuck to the Abbasid
Caliphs even after they were chased from Baghdad by Mongol
armies in 1258. Notwithstanding his success in halting the
Mongol onslaught in the battle of Ain Jalut (1260), the first
Mamluk sultan was killed and replaced by one of his fellow
soldiers. The latter, Baybars (1223, r. 1260–77), propped up his
shaky authority by raising to caliphal dignity a surviving member
of the Abbasid house. Islam's paramount authority now resided in
Cairo, under the tutelage of an upstart dynasty. After the Ottoman
conquest of Cairo in 1517, the relics of the Prophet were brought to
Istanbul. The Ottomans had no place for a puppet Caliph, but
they appropriated the title and used it to their advantage in the
Muslim world.

The spread of Islam not only disseminated the Prophet's religion,
it also brought his real or imagined descendants to distant places.
The wide dispersal of Muhammad's relatives was exceptional, yet
migration was common for many dynasties, who moved from
place to place accumulating titles and territories. Chinggis Khan's

descendants, the Chinggisids, established successor empires in all directions, from Yuan China, Chagatai Central Asia, and Ilkhanid Persia to the Golden Horde dominating Muscovy. The shared Chinggisid legacy, frequently riven by succession struggles, mingled with the diverging religious, cultural, and administrative practices of these areas. In Europe, the intermarriage of monogamous royal houses created a web of entangled succession rights. Partitions and extinctions of senior and junior lines led to a permanent reshuffling of dynastic portfolios, sometimes negotiated peacefully, sometimes enforced by armed contestation. Typically, European kingdoms took shape as an assemblage of duchies and counties under the authority of a prince who recognized rights and privileges of the component parts. Yet families accrued sovereign rights over more distant areas in and beyond Europe. Charles V (1500–58), who reigned as emperor between 1519 and 1556, accumulated seventy-odd titles from the centre to the westernmost fringes of Europe and in the New World. His successors in Madrid and particularly in Vienna held numerous titles, many in areas distant from their main capitals. Ruling a patchwork of realms, they needed to conform to local traditions, speak several languages, accept diverse political conventions, and don different regalia in each realm.

The image of an undying dynasty could become almost synonymous with the country over which it reigned. The Japanese imperial house, entangled with the history of Japan from the legendary Emperor Jimmu (711, r. 660–585 BCE) until the present, is perhaps the most striking example. The bumps and hurdles of dynastic succession were obscured in the genealogy, which made it plausible to present the imperial family as the core element of Japanese continuity. In Africa, the Solomonids form another conspicuous example. The Old Testament describes the visit to King Solomon in Jerusalem by the Queen of Sheba with her splendid cortège. She was one among a number of queens ruling in smaller pre-Islamic Arab principalities. However, the Ethiopian Solomonids (1270–1974) appropriated her legacy by presenting themselves as the descendants of Solomon and the Queen of Sheba. The story was important for the rulers as well as for a wider public: a European traveller noted that Ethiopian King Iyasu II (1723, r. 1730–55) always wore a golden locket around his neck containing his cherished biblical genealogy. The Ottomans and the Habsburgs can be cited as dynasties whose remarkable longevity rendered them almost synonymous with the territories they ruled. It is difficult to think about the history of Turkey and Austria without taking into account these ruling houses.

Alternatively, individual families could be subsumed in an overarching royal or imperial tradition. Rome and Byzantium, where heredity was never the only criterion for succession, were governed by a series of short-lived dynasties. The Roman imperial tradition held greater charisma than every single succeeding house. The legacy of Roman caesars, closely connected to conquest and imperial grandeur, was cultivated in Byzantium, in the successor-states of Charlemagne's empire, and in Moscow. When in 1547 Ivan the Terrible (1533, r. 1547–84) adopted the title of tsar, he relied on a story tracing the descent of Muscovite princes to Emperor Augustus. The titles 'tsar' and 'Kaiser' were both copied from caesar. Almanacs in Habsburg Vienna portrayed the ruling emperor as successor of the Roman caesars. Charlemagne, Charles V, and Napoleon all re-enacted their Roman imperial status in carefully choreographed coronations in the presence of the Roman pontiff. Emperors who gained power through conquest invariably positioned themselves in pre-existing genealogies of imperial power. These traditions did not always stop at geopolitical boundaries. After Charles V's imperial coronation in 1530, Süleyman had himself depicted with an elaborate headdress comprising the imperial crown, the papal tiara, and an Ottoman war helmet (see Figure 8). Governing from the former capital of the Byzantine Empire, the Ottoman Sultan appropriated Roman and papal grandeur. An inscription in Topkapı palace presented him as 'Sultan of the worlds, Solomon of

8. Ottoman Sultan Süleyman the Magnificent wearing the
jewel-studded crown-tiara-helmet, *c.*1540–50.

his time', adding biblical allusions to the accumulation of titles from East and West.

Like imperial Rome, the Chinese imperial legacy furnished a coherent image of authority exercised in practice by a long string of dynasties each lasting up to several centuries. All dynasties adopted the fundamental accoutrements of traditional Chinese imperial power. Moreover, China could boast greater political continuity than Rome, notwithstanding frequent conquests, rebellions, and divisions. The exemplary rule of legendary sage kings Yao, Shun, and Yu was invoked throughout Chinese history. The deeds and writings of famous emperors, most notably Tang Taizong, were absorbed by newcomers. How did such novices deal with the dynasties immediately preceding their rule? Even before the Manchu Qing dynasty conquered China, it acquired the supposed seal of the Chinggisid Yuan dynasty (1279–1368). Once safely vested in power, the new dynasty presented offerings at the Ming tombs. Following Chinese custom, it now also ordered the history of the Ming dynasty to be compiled. These forms of respect for predecessors underlined the legitimacy of the new ruling house. At the same time, there was no clemency for recalcitrant supporters of the Ming pretender.

A well-documented, comprehensive, but short-lived attempt to consolidate a new ruling house can be found in the recent past: Napoleon. The Corsican general started out as a revolutionary, became a consolidator, and soon coveted the supreme accolade of imperial dignity. In the process he rapidly adopted the trappings of royalty. When in 1801 Napoleon reconciled France with the Catholic Church through the concordat with Pope Pius VII, he also created a group of staunch supporters who were relieved to see their lucrative purchase of confiscated church lands acknowledged by the Pope. Having secured a stable basis in France and a *modus vivendi* with the papacy, the First Consul moved on to acquire imperial and royal dignity. Napoleon vainly tried to obtain the regalia of the Holy Roman Empire, safely stashed away by the Habsburgs. Making do without Charlemagne's crown, Napoleon eclipsed earlier emperors by forcing the Pope to be present at his coronation, while usurping the right to put the crown on his own head. In 1805, moreover, he acquired the prestigious iron crown of Lombardy for his coronation as king of Italy in Milan. The new emperor cherry-picked distinctive items and habits from various traditions to fashion his own palace staff and forms of representation. In addition, he created honorific rewards for soldiers, administrators, and nobles. To his grand-style bricolage of dynastic legacies he added marriage alliances with European royalty, most notably his own second marriage to the Habsburg princess Marie-Louise of Austria. The members of his clan and his most loyal supporters were positioned as monarchs and governors in satellite states. This was a dynasty in the making.

Napoleon did what others had done before him: he established a new order by connecting the charisma of the successful warlord to hallowed traditions. His case might appear to be an exception because the French Revolution so severely dented the foundations of European royalty. Did this turbulent phase of change grant more manoeuvring space to the parvenu emperor? We have to remind ourselves that many new dynasties emerged in long and bloody 'times of troubles'. The neat dates of dynastic changeover hide decades of turmoil, with a ruling dynasty facing rebellion, a successful new pretender gradually amassing force before finally grabbing power. The death toll and destruction of the Ming–Qing changeover in China surpassed by far that of the revolutionary and Napoleonic wars in Europe. All warlords emerging in power after protracted struggles needed to reconstruct an image of legitimate rule. After chasing out rivals and entrenching their supporters, they had to take steps like those of Napoleon: establish a rapport with religious authority, cultivate a link with previous dynastic legacies and local traditions, capture regalia, and win over subjects. For these purposes, it was necessary to set up a majestic household.

Setting up house

Houses demonstrate status. Potentates live in places standing out from their environment. Most modern presidents have official residences, where some of them live with their families. These residences can be eye-catching monumental houses: the White House in Washington and the Élysée palace in Paris come to mind. Alternatively, residences form part of larger complexes, such as the Kremlin in Moscow or the former imperial gardens (Zhongnanhai) in Beijing. In these places a domestic staff caters for the daily needs of leaders; yet at the same time, they are venues for state visits, prestigious banquets, and policy meetings. Residences and their personnel fulfil important functions, but nowadays they form only a negligible portion of the aggregate of government agencies. Those serving the president in person may have some influence, but they are not necessarily ranked among the high and mighty.

The political constellation was proportioned differently in history: the king's abode and household formed the single most important institution. Palaces at the heart of capital cities were tangible signs of royal authority. A string of country palaces for royal outdoor recreation and movement added to the visibility of royalty. In these places, kings lived with their relatives, served by domestics, advisors, and armed retainers who formed the upper echelon of government. The king's personal servants combined their domestic duties with leadership in army and government. All sovereign households comprised personnel catering for sleep and procreation; eating and hospitality; mobility, hunt, and warfare. Sleeping quarters housed treasures, and chamberlains hence took charge of movable wealth. Table servants supervised provisioning and held responsibility for the economy of house and realm. Stables were connected to the military and marshals led the way in the army and at court. Chamberlains, stewards, and marshals frequently met the king, and could regulate the admission of others. This was particularly relevant for the chamberlain, gatekeeper to the royal sleeping quarters. Dignitaries responsible for devotion, rites, and sacrifices did not always form part of the household, yet these activities were of central importance.

The attire of servants and the splendour of palaces signalled wealth and authority. They provided the prince with a platform to celebrate dignified rites, to receive on a grand scale, and to distribute largesse. Palaces attracted remarkable numbers of servants, friends, visitors, and petitioners: the inflation of the establishment around princes was one way of redistributing wealth. In African kingdoms, numerous representatives of villages, crafts, and social groups flocked to the court; by accepting hospitality or office, they became stakeholders of the dynastic venture. Wife-giving and polygyny further inflated the numbers: a huge harem demonstrated the king's virility and fertility, and at the same time created bonds with families across the realm.

Not only did these establishments coincide with government: they were a conspicuous presence in society. The Abomey palace of the Leopard Kings of Dahomey, in modern-day Benin, numbered an estimated 5,000 to 8,000 persons, mostly women. Around 1700 this represented between 1 and 2 per cent of the total population. Kingdoms elsewhere in Africa, too, had huge royal establishments for relatively small populations. Royal courts in greater kingdoms and empires were even larger in absolute numbers, yet far less impressive as a share of the populations. The Ottoman court at its height numbered around 13,000 staff out of an estimated population of twenty-five million. Louis XIV's court, the largest of all European royal establishments, numbered 15,000 domestics, officers, and elite soldiers, in a French population of around twenty million. These courts added up to less than 0.1 per cent of their populations. The late Ming court trumped the Ottomans and Bourbons by several thousand, but represented an even tinier fraction of the huge Chinese population.

Even in these larger kingdoms and empires, however, the household occupied a dominant place in government. Armies formed by far the largest institutions everywhere, but they consisted mostly of common foot soldiers, distant from court and government. Almost universally the household was the second-largest institution. The specialized administrative services so powerfully present in modern states followed only in the third place. These government agencies developed as offshoots of the household, when paperwork or the technicalities of finance and justice demanded trained clerks. Some examples diverge from this general pattern. In Rome the emperor's household was added to an already existing republican state structure, in which it remained a somewhat incongruous element. Imperial China's bureaucracy was separated at an early stage from the domestic establishment around the emperor, and soon matched or even outgrew it. Moreover, the learned magistrates enjoyed a higher status than the eunuchs (castrated men) predominating in household service.

Elsewhere, staffs of clerks were relatively small and mostly subservient to domestic dignitaries. Pen-pushing clerks were prominent in West and South Asia long before they occupied centre stage in Europe: yet overall, royal households were larger than bureaucracies. From the later Middle Ages onwards, financial and legal institutions moved out of the European court, rose in numbers, and developed a corporate identity. However, the central state institutions in France, even after the intense phase of centralization in the 17th century, numbered 600 to 800 officials—fewer than the domestics serving Louis XIV's brother, let alone the king's own far more numerous household. From the 1760s onwards, drastic budget cuts in the household, coinciding with the gradual expansion of government services, started to shift the balance between household and government in most European countries.

Palaces accommodated very dissimilar groups. Polygyny entailed the presence of several hundred or more women, who were supervised most often by eunuchs. Women and eunuchs occupied palace sections inaccessible to male visitors whatever their rank. Only in this way could the paternity of the ruler be safeguarded. The sleeping quarters of rulers would be located in or close to these inner domains. A spatial divide between a secluded female inner area and a more accessible male outer area characterized polygynous courts. 'Inner' and 'outer' court groups had different opportunities to manipulate the sovereign: in the council or during excursions in daytime; wining, dining, and snuggling in the evening and night. A 17th-century French visitor reported that at the Persian court: 'the Prime Minister has a hard game to play, for the Favourite Eunuchs and the Sultanesses annul and cancel in the night whatever orders he makes in the day time.' Rivalry among ambitious concubines or councillors could lead to alliances across the spatial divide, yet friction between inner and outer domains persisted. Chinese magistrates deplored the influence of concubines and eunuchs; they accused these inner-court people of corrupting rulers and undermining harmony. The same stance can be found among the people of the pen in West and South Asia. In monogamous Christian Byzantium, eunuchs likewise had obtained a reputation for venomous scheming. A chronicler stated: 'when a viper bit a eunuch, it was the viper that died.'

The spatial divide along gender lines was far less rigid in monogamous Europe. Princes as well as princesses were served by overwhelmingly male households, yet all princesses in addition employed lower-ranking female servants, noble girls, and senior women officeholders in their inner chambers. In fact, kings often recruited their paramours from among the ladies serving their spouses. There was an ongoing attempt to shield the younger girls in particular from the gaze of male courtiers, through strict rules and surveillance. Nevertheless, there was movement between male and female spaces. High-ranking males were allowed to enter the quarters of kings, but also visited the contiguous apartments of their spouses. Even in the absence of a wholly secluded inner domain, noble court dignitaries and learned officials frequently expressed their concerns about the iniquitous dealings of mistresses and low-ranking chamber servants—the closest European equivalents of eunuchs—if they assumed these to hold sway over the sovereign.

Domestics, soldiers, clerics, and administrators converged in the households of kings worldwide. These functions were performed by groups of different social status: princes, nobles, educated scholars, free commoners, and slaves. Slaves and freedmen serving as domestics or administrators were a common occurrence in palaces. Turkic slave soldiers (called *ghulams* or *mamluks*) serving the Abbasids soon rose to leading positions. Later waves of migrating Turkic warriors formed their own dynasties. The ultimate form of slave power was reached under the Mamluks of Cairo (1250–1517), where military slaves could rise in one generation to the supreme office of Sultan. Ottoman sultans employed slaves at all levels and in all capacities, as concubines, pages, domestics, soldiers, governors, and viziers—though not as scholars of Holy Law.

Hierarchy and descent were of prime importance at many courts; yet at the same time, the disenfranchised could outmanoeuvre grandees in the competition for positions of power. Social and religious outcasts, slaves, and foreigners fulfilled important functions in the vicinity of the ruler. Marginality appeared to guarantee loyal subservience and hence made possible the ruler's trust and intimacy. High rank, conversely, might prevent easy camaraderie with sovereigns and complicate careers in government. Not without reason, kings feared that scions of vested families might be tempted to consider their own interests before executing royal directives. Outsiders acquired easy access to the prince; high nobles held social prestige on the basis of their birth rank; magistrates, finally, dominated in hierarchies defined by learning, specialized skills, and office. Only rarely did a single group dominate the three hierarchies of access, birth rank, and government office. Occasionally, examples can be found of social climbers, who, through the king's favour, raced through the ranks of office and status. Their pre-eminence, however, was usually short-lived: many favourites died violently or behind bars.

The persistent tensions between different groups and individuals at court made it tempting for kings to rule by dividing. They could use the scramble for favours to their advantage, by promoting loyal dependants and snubbing haughty dignitaries. Like modern leaders and managers, sovereigns thought twice before heaping bonuses on the shoulders of overly ambitious principals, whereas they found it easier to reward the loyalty and competence of subordinate staff. However, active meddling with hierarchies risked inciting vested interests against the crown and could end in uncontainable strife. Only perceptive as well as strong-minded kings could confidently manage this high-risk strategy, which could turn against them in old age, or under their less astute successors. Founder-emperors, grabbing power in times of troubles, redesigned social hierarchies with impunity while they restored order. This opportunity would recur in reduced form at the beginning of new reigns. Longer interregnums, even under an established ruling house, coincided with fierce competition: restoration made room for changes in hierarchies and offices.

Divide-and-rule was typically used by strong figures in times of turmoil; alternatively, it arose as a hazardous defensive response of princes to the challenge posed by increasingly demanding elites. Maintaining cohesion and purpose in the upper layers was the high road towards royal success, manipulating rivalry a hazardous but effective short-term instrument to get rid of defiant servants. Eventually, rulers were best served by achieving a reputation as bringers of equity and order.

Performing kingship

Dynastic rule has left a huge cultural footprint. Kings sponsored magnificent palaces, a rich literary and musical culture, and an immense variety of art works—often at great cost. The artistic legacies of the dynastic past persist today, but the ephemeral shows of rulership are no longer visible for modern audiences. Yet the design and performance of festive and solemn celebrations ranked among the highest priorities of rulers and involved leading court artists. New kings were expected to create ties with their populations through a series of public performances. The onset of reigns was marked by visits to tombs of previous rulers, prayer at holy places, and initiation rituals. All pre-modern rulers spent time on annually recurring cycles of rituals: Chinese Grand Sacrifices, the Christmas and Easter cycles in Christendom, the Breaking of the Fast and the Sacrifice Feast in Islam. These celebrations made visible the link between rulers and religious observance. Dynastic births, birthdays, marriages, and deaths formed another common occasion for festivity. The circumcision signalling the majority of the Sultan's sons emerged as the most lavish festival in the Ottoman Empire. Twice a year, on their birthdays according to the lunar and solar calendars, Mughal rulers and their sons were publicly weighed (see Figure 9), with jewellery and gold piled up on the scales. On the occasion of these festivals amnesties were announced and the poor received charity.

Foreign envoys entered the capital and were received at court with great splendour. Their missions showed the prestige of the prince among his fellow-rulers. Royals themselves travelled through their realms: they inspected cities, greeted dignitaries, listened to reports, dispensed justice, and granted amnesties. Hunting expeditions and military manoeuvres led to more mobility and encounters. Finally, daily life at court entailed a series of ritualized encounters with officials, soldiers, and incidental visitors. Religious observance, dynastic demography, and encounters in the realm and at court structured the calendar of princes with a series of ritual obligations. The mantle of royalty needed to be earned in ongoing performance after having been gained on the battlefield.

9. Emperor Jahangir weighing his son Prince Khurram against gold and silver, 1615 (British Museum, London 1948,1009,0.69).

Not all kings were equally burdened, neither were their burdens equally proportioned. In China, towering ritual demands centring on the emperor went together with the inaccessibility of the incumbent. The grand sacrifices were performed in seclusion among a small circle of magistrates; the population knew about the rites, but did not witness them. In East Asia, kings could perform their roles as protectors of the people and moral exemplars without encountering their subjects. The balance was different in West and South Asia and in Europe. Islam and Christianity demanded some form of contact between rulers and the population. Processions to Friday Prayer or Mass typically formed occasions for petitioning: in the eyes of God, all were equal. Religion reminded rulers of their humility; active government and military command, moreover, necessitated contact. Conversely, Christian and Islamic kings could leave some of the moral burdens carried by their East-Asian fellow-rulers on the shoulders of religious specialists.

The trade-off between isolation and interaction depended not only on regional conventions: dispositions of individual sovereigns made a difference. Outgoing characters in East Asia detested the imposition of confinement and isolation, whereas introspective personalities elsewhere shied away from the encounters forced on them. Consecutive dynasties and individuals developed their own idiom of interactions, yet their advisors would remind them of the responsibilities conventionally attached to sovereign office. Disregarding cultural preferences and ignoring ritual obligations could jeopardize the survival of dynasties.

Elites flocked to the centre during the highlights in the ritual calendar not only to watch the show or meet their equals: they also hoped to obtain benefits. Governments assemble and dispense wealth; mete out punishments and rewards; define hierarchies and promote or demote their servants. Kings stood at the heart of this machinery and ideally assured its equity as well as its swiftness. Even-handed distribution of honours was vital for effective rule. It drew candidates and petitioners to the centre and created loyal supporters throughout the realm. This was the opportunity for new kings to attract support among the elites and attach them to the dynastic venture.

All layers of the population were in theory able to petition the sovereign, during moments of interaction, typically around religious observances, or through written procedures. Some kings actively invited their subjects to complain about the agents of royal power. Protecting victims and punishing wrongdoers, kings obtained a double advantage: the populace might admire their justness, while leading servants noticed to their dismay how their hidden dealings unexpectedly could be unveiled and subjected to royal scrutiny. Nevertheless, kings and elites well understood their mutual dependence. Individuals could be punished, but without the active support of regional elites, no government would survive. Conversely, the benefits distributed by the sovereign were a great boost for elites.

Pre-modern kingdoms and empires comprised clusters of hierarchies driven by loyalty, service, and the expectation of benefits. Like modern chosen representatives eager to generate support among their constituencies, regional elites needed access to the boons of the realm to satisfy their followers. The patrons themselves competed for the king's favours and promised loyal support in return. By attaching these intermediaries to the royal court, kings and their advisors could consolidate dynastic power. The leaders of elite networks performed the same feats at the regional level, by assembling supporters in their households and co-opting high-ranking associates through marriage alliances. Bonds created by household service, kinship, and affinity were vital for political cohesion at all levels. In many cases there was little procedure or administration in local government beyond this pyramid of patronage. Moreover, even highly organized bureaucracies with fixed written procedures still heavily relied on loyalties created through personal contact and the exchange of gifts and services. Neither was this necessarily inefficient: as long as kings could stand unchallenged at the pinnacle of the pyramid, they could hope to rule with a light touch, preventing frequent eruptions of rebellion and repression.

In China, the ruling imperial clan formed the only acknowledged dynasty, apart from the descendants of Confucius. Numerous lineages of gentlemen-scholars successfully maintained their status by combining landed wealth with learning and government office. From the Song dynasty onwards, however, candidates for office needed to pass through highly demanding civil service examinations. European Jesuits noted the absence of a European-style hereditary nobility in Ming China and expressed their admiration for the intricate machinery of the examinations. The Qing dynasty introduced Manchu and Mongol nobles into the heart of the government, but confirmed the examination system as the main conduit for bureaucratic office. Temporary nobility was granted in recognition of outstanding service in government and army. Full hereditary nobility was restricted to the Manchu-Mongol conquest clan, governing most of the newly conquered peripheral lands. In the heartlands of China, government compounds showed the face of imperial authority, but these miniature palaces were the headquarters of magistrates rather than the domiciles of noble dynasties.

Conversely, Europe formed a hierarchy of royal and noble dynasties, each with its own court or household. Kings ruled their countries under the nominal authority of the emperor; a pyramid of nobles administered their domains in each kingdom. Hereditary noble power was equated to a large extent with 'natural' authority, for kings, as the first gentlemen of their kingdoms, as well as for the nobles in their realm. Noble houses retained their importance during the rapid expansion and social promotion of administrative hierarchies, and lasted even beyond the watershed of the French Revolution. In Europe, dynasty was never solely the remit of kings and emperors: it entailed a shared language of hereditary elite status. Social climbers adopted a noble way of life, concluded marriage alliances among nobles, and created impressive genealogies. The influx of new wealth strengthened nobilities and thus assisted the remarkable persistence of noble ideology.

Other regions stand between these two cases. The Ottomans from the 16th century onwards were governed largely by a military-administrative class recruited as slaves. Nevertheless, leading servants of the House of Osman rapidly acquired the grandee outlook befitting their occupations: advising the sultan in the council, leading fleets and armies, or governing provinces. Their households became increasingly important as a source of new recruits for government office in the course of the 17th century. Heredity of status among pasha and vizier families, moreover, increased in the 18th century. Dependants of slave origin gradually turned into an entrenched elite. Leading officeholders in Safavid Persia and Mughal India likewise turned from dependants into elites. Safavid religious devotees became vested regional governors; Mughal officeholders depending on centrally regulated hierarchies of payment and status increasingly acted as independent powerholders. Even before this process gathered force, these groups resembled Europe's noble elites with their retinues and splendid living quarters.

Chapter 5
Persistence and change

The dynastic cycle

Most ancient empires and kingdoms used dynasties and individual reigns as building blocks of their chronologies. The reckoning of time was entangled with king lists: without knowledge of reigns and names history made no sense. Typically, in the earliest visions of history, divinity and kingship were intertwined with the origins of the realm. All peoples have used the returning patterns of days and seasons to structure their lives. Many built annual calendars around their observations of sun and moon, and construed longer-lasting cycles on the movement of planets, stars, and comets. Regnal dates formed the most common way of naming and ordering these recurring annual cycles. The advent of new religions inserted a point zero in calendars: years were counted from this moment onwards, yet this represented a shift in priority rather than the disappearance of regnal dating.

The never-ending listing of kings imparted the view of an unbroken chain with the past, but at the same time it suggested the repeated rise and fall of ruling houses. Did dynasties necessarily follow the organic trajectory of birth, growth, maturity, old age, and death? A cyclical view of dynastic power can be found in the naming of kings. King lists from Rwanda to Tenochtitlan and beyond show a limited number of traditional names given to royalty, referring to the position of these kings in a repeating cycle. Such titles were spokes in the wheel of sacralized dynastic power rather than individual names; their repeated sequence conveys a worldview presented in the form of a historical chronicle.

Many pre-modern political thinkers viewed the world as a place of steady decay, and defined a golden age in the past rather than in the future. Model rulers were placed in a distant past, where morals and religion were still untainted. The legendary first Chinese rulers Yao, Shun, and Yu served as exemplars of good government until the end of imperial China. Sasanian-Persian King Khosrow I (501, r. 531–79) was remembered as a paragon of just rule and magnificence by his distant Persian and Arabic successors. The wisdom and splendour of Solomon likewise enthralled later generations. Ages decaying from gold and silver to bronze and iron figure in Greek and Roman mythology. In the Bible, Daniel explains Nebuchadnezzar II's (634 BCE, r. 605–562 BCE) dream about a statue with a head made of fine gold, chest and arms of silver, stomach and hips of bronze, legs of iron, and feet of clay as the steady regression of empires before the advent of the heavenly kingdom. The coming of a prophet-king, renewing the cycle or inaugurating the end of times, can be found in religious traditions around the world. In the 16th century, Franciscan friars fused their cyclical expectations with those of Aztec sages in a joint rewriting of pre-Columbian history. Messiahs, mahdis, and maitreyas were eagerly expected in Europe and Asia alike.

The idea of degeneration could be phrased more detachedly as an inevitable cycle of healthy and corrupt governments. Plato distinguished a cycle of degeneration in five regimes: aristocracy governed by the philosopher-king, timocracy (with political participation based on property ranks), oligarchy, democracy, and finally, tyranny. Aristotle presented a simpler model of polities ruled by one, few, and many. Leaders ideally acted in the interests of the community, yet the three forms of government could easily degenerate into their selfish forms: tyranny, oligarchy, and mob rule.

The Greek historian Polybius (200–118 BCE) gave yet another variant of Plato's model, starting with monarchy, and moving via tyranny, aristocracy, oligarchy, and democracy to the low ebb of mob rule—chaos would then lead to a fresh start of the same sequence. Mulling over such formulae after almost two millennia, Montesquieu differentiated between republic, monarchy, and despotism, each with its own leading principle. Decay manifested itself as the likely movement from the idealized aristocratic republic based on virtue, to the more practicable form of monarchy directed by the principle of honour, which, however, might in turn degrade into despotism guided by fear.

These alternating phases of decay and rejuvenation could easily be linked to the fate of dynasties. Myriads of ruling houses rising and falling in the course of history have been examined by eager witnesses. Dynasties seemed to follow a fixed pathway, moving from early blossoming to full fruition and finally to decay. The youth of a ruling house came with vigour and purity; maturity brought the unfolding of the full panoply of dynastic grandeur but also exposed the first signals of decline; old age coincided with dilapidation and loss of physical as well as moral strength. By exploiting and abusing the population, rulers in this phase inevitably triggered rebellion, invasion, and downfall. The rise to power of a new house was at the same time a necessary moral rejuvenation of government.

The Chinese historian Sima Qian (145–85 BCE), writing in the century after the advent of the Han dynasty, described how the three dynasties arising in the second millennium BCE, Xia, Shang, and Zhou, started with great virtue yet lost their lustre after several generations. Each dynasty gradually presented a caricature of its own original quality: under the Xia, good faith turned into rusticity; the Shang moved from piety to superstition; with the Zhou refinement and order deteriorated into a 'mere hollow show'. Soon after the forceful rule of the first emperor and unifier of China, Qin Shi Huangdi (259, r. 221–201 BCE), disorders arose from which the first Han emperor reached power. Sima Qian noted that the new dynasty needed to recommence the cycle: 'the way of the Three Dynasties of old is like a cycle which, when it ends must begin over again'. In addition to the cycle of the three early houses, Chinese scholars related the recurring alternation of dynasties to the subsequent rule of the five elements: wood, fire, earth, metal, and water, each with its complement of a colour, a planet, and certain inherent qualities.

The most detailed explanation of the inevitable decay and replacement of dynasties was coined by Ibn Khaldun (1332–1406). In the introduction to his multi-volume world history this North African Muslim scholar argued that as a rule, 'no dynasty lasts beyond the lifespan of three generations'. Each forty-year generation followed its predestined path in the cycle from rise and consolidation to downfall. A dynasty might persist beyond four generations, but only on the brink of ruin and as a shadow of its former grandeur. Rugged nomadic desert tribes were the prime mover of Ibn Khaldun's cycles. These pristine warriors found it easy to overrun decaying urban empires. Inevitably, however, the conquerors succumbed to the luxuries of the palace. Metropolitan life sapped their strengths and fomented rivalry in their ranks. The first two generations of leaders had still known desert life; the founder's example was strong during his successor's reign. The third-generation prince, born and educated in the palace, mimicked tradition without understanding it. Under his reign the dynasty might reach its apogee, but it did so at the cost of losing the connection with its former supporters. Without tribal group solidarity (*asabiyyah*) the dynastic edifice became a house of cards.

More than anything else, the unravelling of tribal group solidarity caused the downfall of dynasties. Why did this always occur? Ibn Khaldun first points to urban sedentary luxuries undermining the valour and morals of the conquerors. In addition, he mentions a familiar concern: the ruler's rivalry with relatives and former stalwarts. These tribal fellow-warriors, alienated by the airs of supremacy affected by their leader, became a threat to his authority. In anticipation, the king might curtail their rights and attract other groups to support his government. During the highpoint of the dynasty, Ibn Khaldun notes, tribal warriors were side-tracked by pen-pushers and mercenaries. Their alienation in the long run undermined the dynasty and exposed it to conquest by an untarnished and unified desert tribe.

The expectation of a downturn in the fate of a dynasty remained strong throughout history in China as well as in West and South Asia. Princes growing up in the luxury and isolation of the palace risked losing 'humility and respect' for their ordinary subjects; they might be tempted to indulge in expensive fancies or useless military ventures, overburdening rather than protecting the people. Exploitation, injustice, and the neglect of proper rituals could invoke the wrath of heaven, manifested by the disobedience of the populace, invasions, and the downfall of the dynasty. Noticing the wrongdoings of his sons, the Ming founder Zhu Yuanzhang (1328, r. 1368–98) anxiously asked himself whether the Mandate of Heaven would now be withdrawn.

His apprehension would be recognized not only by many other emperors, but also by the elites supporting the edifice of dynastic power: how could they prevent degeneration? In the late 16th century, Ottoman learned elites viewed changes in the set-up of dynastic government with grave concern: did the withdrawal of Sultan Murad III (1546, r. 1574–95) into the palace and his subsequent reliance on inner-court favourites announce a downturn along the lines of Ibn Khaldun's model? During the ensuing critical decades of war and revolt, sultans were deposed and reinstated, and there was a first instance of regicide: Osman II (1604, r. 1618–22) was imprisoned and strangled by disgruntled janissaries, the slave-based household infantry elite. Osman II would not be the last sultan to die at the hands of his own servants. Interestingly, the unruly elites did not choose to replace the ruling house. Promoting a candidate from among their own ranks was neither desirable nor perhaps likely to succeed. The prestige of this long-lasting ruling house prevented outright usurpation, but it allowed violent manipulation by elites who purported to act in the interests of people and dynasty.

Chinese views of the dynastic cycle and Ibn Khaldun's model both underline a moral element: forgetting their roots, kings no longer heeded the moral example of their forefathers. Corrupted by the palace, they alienated and exploited their peoples. However, while Chinese scholars identified with the cultural polish of the learned magistracy, Ibn Khaldun makes no secret of his admiration for the brute force of desert peoples. A view akin to that of Ibn Khaldun figured among the dynasties conquering China from the steppe: most notably the Liao (907–1125), Jin (1115–1234), Yuan (1271–1368), and Qing (1636–1912). These dynasties sought a middle way between the Chinese example and their own traditions. Did they fear decline as a consequence of adopting a Chinese lifestyle? The Qing Qianlong emperor (1711, r. 1735–96, abdication 1796, d. 1799) certainly did his best to rekindle valour and loyalty among the Manchus and their Mongol allies. Here, too, group cohesion and the martial tradition were seen as the key to dynastic survival. The ideal in these cases was always to return to the imagined vigour and uprightness of the conquest generation. The cliché of a clash between forceful 'barbarians' and peoples enfeebled by luxury and sophistication can be found in many other stories. The epos of Alexander's conquests includes it as a powerful subplot: the hero's adoption of haughty and luxurious Persian-style kingship aggravated his Macedonian fellows-in-arms.

Behind the moral injunctions of cyclical views, a very practical point becomes visible. Ibn Khaldun, who during the siege of Damascus in 1401 conversed at length with the renowned conqueror Timur (1336, r. 1370–1405), viewed the tribal cohesion of desert tribes as the essential requirement for conquest.

Conquerors shared booty with their supporters and relied on them as loyal agents of government. Yet, once established in power, how could they ensure the lasting compliance and loyalty of these brawny followers? This was a tough challenge: followers became entrenched elites: powers and possessions delegated by royalty changed into family heirlooms. History shows countless versions of this story and its counterpart, the appearance of kings who forcefully reunited autonomous elites under their rule. Waves of centralization alternated with drawn-out phases of involution and sudden moments of violent breakdown and renewal. Shorn of its strong moral overtones, the model of the dynastic cycle can be read as a plausible description of the recurring phases of integration and dissolution, caused by the tensions between rulers and elites.

Dynastic change and variety

The depiction of shared aspects of dynastic power in the preceding chapters should not lead to the faulty assumption that dynasties were timeless and unchanging, or knew only cyclical change. How did scale, change over time, and regional variety impact dynastic power? Some kings ruled over miniature kingdoms without script, operating on the basis of direct contact between governors and governed. At the other extreme, emperors governed huge empires through a multi-tiered bureaucratic machinery relying on written communication. Cultural backgrounds, religious creeds, social structures, and economic practices varied widely. Moreover, major changes took place in every region during the five millennia separating Narmer, the legendary unifier of early Egypt, from Louis XVI on his way to the scaffold in 1793.

The variety of isolated research traditions and the diversity of the sources available make it difficult to present a coherent story about regional differences and change over time. Some remarkable divergences between the major script cultures have been highlighted in the preceding chapters. The ideal of rulership was more martial, outgoing, and active in Europe and West Asia than in East Asia, where the ideal of the inward-looking paragon of morality and learning was stronger. Princes surely did not all fit into the predominant cultural mould, yet their advisors would remind them of their duties. The diverging traditions shaped interaction with the population and the format of palace complexes. More diversity strikes the eye. The norm of monogamous marriage set European dynasties apart from their peers around the globe—this divergent custom helped to create a densely interacting network of competing dynasties unknown elsewhere. It also created a different notion of the family.

The most striking contrasts are to be found in the definition of the family and the forms of succession to supreme royal dignity. Here it becomes clear that scale and government by paper made a difference. No single large-scale empire practised matrilineal descent. Succession through the female line entailed diffusion and choice; father–son succession, frowned upon in many small-scale matrilineal as well as patrilineal African kingdoms, made possible concentration. The logic of fixed father–son succession in the male line became dominant in major kingdoms and empires. Here, continuity and concentration were the prime goal. Diffusion and competition, present in many smaller kingdoms but also in the dynamic expansionist phase of the Ottoman, Mughal, and Safavid empires, were transformed into fixed succession during phases of consolidation. The family was re-defined to fit this priority: junior branches were curtailed. Families were subjugated to the control of the ruler—or, perhaps, his advisors. Indeed, the strengthening of central powers often went hand in hand with a reduced impact of individual rulers, who were themselves increasingly bound by fixed procedures and elaborate institutions of government.

The increasing predominance of fixed hereditary succession contrasts sharply with the prevalence of election and acclamation in early kingship. Ideally, rulers were selected on the basis of their qualities, as moral guides, war leaders, or nominees of Heaven.

Surely they were expected to come from a distinguished lineage: most eligibles would share a distant ancestor. Yet the final choice would reside in a broader group of kingmakers, which would acclaim its favourite candidate as ruler. The ideal of election by an inner group was strong in early European kingship, where relatively open forms of descent created a pool of candidates rather than a single heir-apparent. The more fixed forms of succession emerging gradually in most realms from the later Middle Ages onwards reduced choice and transformed election into ceremonial acclamation by peers. Islamic political thinkers had reservations about hereditary succession and particularly objected to father–son succession without the seal of public assent. The Umayyad appropriation of the caliphate never sat easily with them. Stories about the Chinese sage kings Yao, Shun, and Yu invariably relate that these exemplars moved to the throne on the express invitation of the people: they underlined the absence of hereditary succession before the rise of the Xia dynasty.

Several conflicting but persisting tendencies can be found throughout dynastic history. Supreme office, acquired through force and talent by a founding figure, tended to become hereditary. The absence of competition and choice in the long run necessarily brought indifferent characters to the throne, incompatible with the qualities attributed to royal paramountcy. Kingship could not easily retain its special quality through fixed hereditary succession; yet open succession entailed bloody phases of changeover. In most cases, dynastic renewal took shape through violence: few lasting forms of peaceful yet competitive succession to supreme power can be traced in history. Kingdoms in which the well-oiled machinery of government could operate with a king who served as a figurehead rather than as an active leader were perhaps best prepared to weather the storms of history.

This trajectory of development leaves open many questions. How can we explain that the sacredness of rulers was most obvious in many small-scale African kingdoms as well as in imperial China, located at the extremes of political consolidation? Perhaps an explanation can be found in the personal responsibilities of the king in sacrifices and rituals? The stature of established religions and the powerful presence of religious specialists may have reduced this burden in other regions. Nevertheless, the sacred dimension of dynastic rule was never restricted to a moment in time, a stage in development, or a specific region. It fitted age-old ideas about the awesome powers of kings, froze the incumbents to immobility, helped to transfix distant audiences, and in practice often placed control in the hands of an inner ring of servants or ministers. Everywhere deeply held beliefs about royalty, hierarchy, and cosmology formed the bedrock of dynastic power. Only the erosion of such beliefs could take away the raison d'être of dynasties. This process first took shape in Europe, and followed elsewhere in the wake of European military hegemony.

European hegemony and modernity

Did cycles transform into a gradual upward movement? The repeated story of rise and fall at some point was replaced by a narrative of long-term consolidation, first and foremost in Europe, but also in Asian empires. History was now seen as a gradual process of consolidating and reinforcing powers in the hands of the prince and central administrative elites, who proved able to enhance their dominion over distant regions. Cycles appeared as minor oscillations only in a narrative of long-term growth.

The history of Europe from the 12th century onwards, punctured and transformed by the Great Plague of the mid-14th century, shows the consolidation of competing kingdoms. Growing economies, specialized government institutions, and increasing royal revenues nurtured Europe's capacity for military confrontation. Likewise, the history of China from the Tang dynasty via the Song to the Yuan and, particularly, to the two late imperial dynasties can be read as a story of gradual consolidation of the powers of the emperor and his magistracy, notwithstanding the recurrence of bloody dynastic changeovers. The Qing governed an empire that was larger, richer, and more densely inhabited than any of its predecessors. Japan under the Tokugawa Shoguns, likewise, showed greater stability and growth than its predecessors. While the cultural refinements of earlier dynasties could still be admired as peerless, they did not match the economic and political performance of their early modern counterparts. In the 16th century the Ottomans briefly emerged as a global maritime player, controlling the Black Sea as well as the Eastern Mediterranean, and attracting the allegiance of allies in the Indian Ocean and the South-East Asian Archipelago. Conquerors of Constantinople, Belgrade, and Baghdad, the Ottomans controlled a huge empire, comprising the capitals of several previous rivals. At the height of their power, the Mughals and Safavids, too, could view their achievements as exceeding those of earlier ruling houses.

This protracted shared Eurasian phase of consolidation and expansion corresponded with the turn towards fixed hereditary succession and concentration of power. Gradually, however, Europe gained military pre-eminence. The ongoing violent competition of European states coincided with their increased global presence as conquerors, traders, and missionaries. The overthrow of the Aztec and Inca empires by the Spaniards opened the American continent for exploitation. Trading posts and fortresses along the coasts of Africa and Asia introduced Europeans in leading roles as conquerors or allies: inevitably, the local political and economic situation was henceforth tied to the presence of Europeans. The wealth and power of slave-trading kings in West Africa was a consequence of globalization at the hands of Europeans.

European expansion did not leave untouched even the great land empires of West, South, and East Asia. At the turn of the 17th century, the Mughals witnessed the erosion of their central powers; by the end of the 18th century, they had come under the tutelage of the British East India Company. After a series of military defeats between 1683 and 1718, Ottoman Sultans could no longer pose as the supreme arbiters of their relationship with European powers; they were forced to conform to European-style diplomacy and adopt a more docile posture. In the course of the 19th century, the Europeans—and by that time also the Americans—started to infringe on Qing China and Tokugawa Japan. The series of breakthroughs occurring in Europe from the later Middle Ages onwards had pushed the most successful contenders in this western tip of the Eurasian continent to global supremacy. In the course of the 18th and 19th centuries it became clear that maintaining or regaining independence required the adoption of European-style innovations, not least in the military.

At the same time Europe itself underwent profound changes in religion, culture, and economy as well as in its political set-up. A straightforward long-term process of de-sacralization of kingship cannot be found in any of the script cultures before the end of the early modern age. In fact, the ceremonial apparatus of kingship in Europe became more conspicuous in the course of the 16th and 17th centuries; notwithstanding their grave hesitations about sacraments, even Protestant courts followed the general tendency. By the late 17th century, however, change was underway, and in the course of the 18th century princes themselves openly took distance from their semi-sacral status.

In 1786 Habsburg Emperor Joseph II (1741, r. 1780–90), the most outspoken of modernizers, scribbled a note to his high steward explaining that he wanted to abolish the reverence on bended knee, a sign of respect he viewed as 'unnecessary between humans, and reserved for God alone'. Joseph abolished religious ceremonies at court in Vienna; yet he entertained an exalted view of his own responsibilities as leader of the state. Somewhere in the changeover to our modern world, the powers of kingship, vested temporarily in a person of flesh and blood, were transferred to the untouchable king's depersonalized successor: the sovereign state.

Royals now presented themselves as officials of the new idol; with their ministers and administrators they came and went, whereas the state endured. Traditionally, the highest moral-religious sanction of kingship was tied to the fortunes of the people. The modern view of popular sovereignty no longer needs a king or emperor, but it restates an old truth by accepting the well-being of the people as its main underpinning. Could royals, divested of their religious sanction and magical allure, survive in the newly designed sovereign state?

Kings and dynasties persist even today; nevertheless, somewhere along the road their place changed irreversibly. Throughout dynastic history, myriads of kings were killed and multiple dynasties were toppled—yet almost always they were replaced by others of their kind. Change was effected not by abolishing kingship or dynastic succession, but by installing a new ruling house. The Italian city states emerging from the overlordship of pope and emperor constitute an exception, yet most of them adopted forms of dynastic rule or were engulfed by dynastic conquest. The venerable republic of Venice stuck to its elaborate electoral system but did place prestige in the figure of the Doge. Abjuring their overlord in the late 16th century, the Dutch initially tried to find a suitably royal replacement, but in the long run they embraced a form of republican government topped by a semi-hereditary stadholder as well as by office-holding families. Even after the momentous execution of the king Charles I in 1649, kingship re-emerged and thrived in England. In the course of the 18th century, fundamental questions were raised about all aspects of the old regime. Many extolled the example of classical republicanism, yet few commended a wholesale change of monarchy. Only during the French Revolution did a new image of the future appear, where the nation no longer needed a ruling house. Typically, the abolition of monarchy and the execution of Louis XVI went together with a backlash against established religion and priesthood. The French revolutionary calendar, defining 22 September 1792 as the first day of year I of the

Republic, weeded out all the Christian elements in the old calendar. It shows what the revolutionaries envisaged: the calendar was not meant as a new turn of the dynastic wheel, but as the solemn inauguration of a profoundly new era, guided by new precepts and ideas.

When in 1799 Napoleon came to power, he presented the first constitution of the consulate as the confirmation of the Revolution's main principles, but also as the end of disorders. Indeed, re-establishing order was Napoleon's first priority, and he abolished several revolutionary innovations—including the calendar. Yet the Revolution had changed the face of Europe. Everywhere, dynasties were under pressure to redefine themselves. The lighthearted political and religious speculation of enlightened freethinkers was obliterated. Conservatism emerged as a conscious force, whereas it had been a traditional reflex before. Restored and redesigned monarchies clashed with radical opponents: in this polarized world, there were harsh choices to be made. Dynasties of all eras had continuously adjusted their representations as well as their interactions with their peoples. In the 19th century, however, new political challenges and changing media of contact made these adjustments more urgent, profound, and conscious. Moreover, Europe's global ascendancy put under pressure dynasties across the globe, who were now caught between their traditional idioms and the forms imposed by the conspicuous success of the new hegemon. Royalty worldwide would undergo the impact of modernization first and foremost in the shape of European military and commercial dominance.

Chapter 6
The dynastic impulse in the modern world

Ruling houses: inflation and adaptation

The turbulent decades around 1800 did not spell the end of dynasty, but they carried the message that alternative forms of power might in the long run gain ascendancy. While royal legitimacy was now openly contested, republics still remained the exception in Europe and worldwide. In 1914, only France, Switzerland, and Portugal (since 1910) ranked as republics among Europe's polities. By that time the most famous early modern republics, Venice and the United Provinces, had disappeared. Venice was first gobbled up by the newly founded Austrian empire, then integrated into the unified Italian monarchy. The Dutch Republic became a kingdom under Napoleon's brother Louis in 1806 and was ruled after 1813 by the dynasty of Orange-Nassau, rising from the stadholderate to full kingship. The revolutionary Belgians, breaking free from Dutch tutelage in 1830–1, chose to establish a kingdom rather than a republic. During the 19th century, new kings rose to power most conspicuously in South-Eastern Europe following the Ottoman retreat. German ruling houses, the house of Saxe-Coburg in particular, provided kings for several new kingdoms.

Conversely, in the Americas republics became the rule, with the United States in the North and numerous new republics burgeoning in the South after the end of Spanish rule. The single longer-lasting instance of dynastic rule here was the Empire of Brazil (1822–89), under a junior branch of the Portuguese Braganza house. Of course, British and Dutch colonial possessions in the Americas formed part of a monarchy—some of them still do today.

The First World War terminated the rule of several European dynasties, most notably the Habsburgs, the Hohenzollerns, and the Romanovs; China and Korea had by that time already ousted their ruling houses, and Turkey would follow soon. Winston Churchill's fear, shared by many in the years between the two world wars, that this was only the start of a 'holocaust of crowns' proved to be erroneous. A surprising number of ruling houses rose to power, in North Africa, West Asia, and later also in South-East Asia, most frequently under British colonial protection.

The breakdown of empires led to the creation of new states, many of them monarchies. Ottoman weakness made possible the rise of dynasties in Africa and Arabia as well as in Europe. During the later 18th century, the Saudi emirs had established themselves in the arid heartlands of the Arabian Peninsula: their march to power would coincide with a ringing appeal to purify Islam. Profiting from Ottoman fragility, the viceroys of Egypt established themselves as semi-independent royals, before the British assumed control in 1882. Kings of Egypt would persist in uncomfortable co-rule with their British masters until the revolt of 1952 established Nasser's republic. During the war against the Ottomans, the British promised to support the Arab bid for independence. In 1916 the sharif of Mecca, proud descendant of the prophet's tribe, proclaimed himself king of the Hejaz. This western maritime strip of the Arabian Peninsula containing the holy cities of Mecca and Medina was soon conquered by the Saudi emirs. In the later 20th century, the Saudi kingdom, boosted by oil wealth and international alliances, became a strong regional power. The sharifs, ousted from Mecca, briefly ruled Syria (1920), enjoyed a longer career as kings of Iraq (1921–58), but stayed in power only as kings of Jordan.

Paradoxically many royal houses emerged as a consequence of the gradual reshaping of the British colonial empire into spheres of influence. British statesmen, including Churchill, viewed dynastic power as the safest option for states under their protection. The Brits spawned monarchies in North Africa and around the Arabian Peninsula. Several of these kingdoms had older roots, but they were all redefined by their relationship with the British. In the decades following the Second World War nationalist rebellions replaced kings with presidents in Egypt (1952), Tunisia (1957), Iraq (1958), Yemen (1962), and Libya (1969). By the time of these republican takeovers the smaller Gulf states had turned from British protectorates into independent states ruled by princes with their extended families. After the Shah of Iran's downfall in 1979 dynastic rule in this part of the world remained remarkably stable. The Arab Spring (2010–12) led to rebellion and regime change in many republics, but rocked only Bahrain among the monarchies in the region. In South-East Asia, Malaysia and Brunei were the last two dynastic regimes to escape from under the British colonial umbrella, obtaining sovereignty and their modern form respectively in 1957/65 and 1984. On a more modest level, the French colonial venture also gave rise to resurgent monarchies in North Africa and South-East Asia. Morocco's Alawi dynasty and Cambodia's house of Norodom had ruled before the coming of the French, but emerged again as kings after the withdrawal of the French in 1956 and 1953, respectively.

Clearly, European colonial powers were an important force in shaping modern monarchies throughout the world, first by maintaining in power local princes under metropolitan control; second through their policies during decolonization. In the process, Europeans impressed their standards on local powerholders. Even countries escaping direct control, such as Japan,

Thailand, Iran (Persia) and Ethiopia (briefly occupied by Italy 1935–41), were profoundly influenced by the European challenge.

Colonial administrators transported their rules and laws to distant countries. They had little patience with the disturbances engendered by contested succession; descent through the female line and diffusion through 'sideways' succession were slowly pushed out. Neither did they see reasons to manage African female reign mates in addition to male paramount chiefs and kings. Missionaries, at the same time, worked hard to spread Christianity and to impose monogamy on rulers as well as on their subjects. Their efforts were only partially crowned with success. Polygyny remained the rule for Muslim princely houses and was not uncommon among elites and princes elsewhere. Moreover, male primogeniture, predominant in Europe as well as in the largest empires of Asia, was never universally embraced. Most of the Arab Gulf dynasties and the Saudis retain a relatively flexible form of succession, mixing pedigree with designation of the heir by the incumbent prince or a family council. A modernized form of election and circulation forms the basis of rule in Malaysia: every five years, the nine hereditary rulers of the Federation's component states choose a king from among their midst.

Conversely, European monarchies incidentally looked to the colonies to find arguments for their own choices. When in 1890 Dutch King William III died without male offspring, a debate arose about the future of the Dutch monarchy. Advocates of his daughter Wilhelmina pointed to the phenomenon of the 'male daughter' in the South-East Asian archipelago, who by temporarily fulfilling the male role could secure the continuity of the house. In fact, Wilhelmina would be succeeded by two queens from the house of Orange-Nassau. Three subsequent generations of male spouses played subdued roles only: paradoxically, queens helped to reproduce and represent a patrilineal dynasty. Women were not to be found in the assemblies and ministries thriving in

19th-century Europe: these were all-male institutions. However, the expansion of state institutions did not affect the possibility of women ascending to the throne: royal blood still enabled them to play major roles. We refer to the 19th century as the 'Victorian Age' not only because Queen-Empress Victoria (1819, r. 1837–1901) ruled for a substantial part of the century and governed over an empire without peers—she also made an impact.

Apart from European constitutional monarchies, two enduring clusters of dynastic rule strike the eye, the first in the region from Morocco to the Persian Gulf (eight monarchies) and the second from Bhutan, Thailand, and Cambodia, to Malaysia and Brunei (five monarchies, not counting Nepal, a republic since 2008). The house of the Prophet Muhammad is prominently present in this listing: Morocco, Jordan, Brunei, and several of the ruling houses in Malaysia cultivate this pedigree. The rise of the Saudis, too, has had a notable religious dimension. Likewise, the legacy of Buddhist sage kings is strong in South Asia, from Bhutan to Thailand. A charismatic religious aura may have helped these clusters of dynasties to survive into modernity—yet no king could without further ado brandish the traditional idiom of kingship.

All kings employed the past as a repository of traditions and artefacts, yet they invariably needed to recreate the foundations of their rule, adapt to changing conditions, and learn how to use new instruments of power. In Europe the expanded state apparatus, frequent elections, and vociferous representative bodies created a new political balance. The royal court now was only one of several foci of power, and not necessarily always the most important. Notwithstanding the great variety in constitutional settlements, all monarchs worldwide had to take into account stronger state institutions and representative bodies as well as an expanding press and public sphere. Moreover, where kings actually held the reins of government in their hands, modern technology, infrastructure, and media made them far more powerful than their dynastic precursors.

Outside of Europe, royalty performed a hazardous tightrope act. On the one hand, royals needed to defend tradition against European incursions; on the other hand, they faced opposition from local nationalist modernizers with republican ideals. Kings could act as national liberators and modernizers, yet popular support might depend equally on their traditional religious role. The balance between modernity and tradition changed according to political contingency and personalities, but the persistent relevance of religious legitimation seems to be typical for most monarchies enduring outside of Europe. Neither did the religious component necessarily weaken over time. Both iconic long-reigning Thai kings, Chulalongkorn (1853, r. 1868–1910) and his grandson Bhumibol (1927, r. 1946–2016), have been represented as Buddhist sage kings. However, the ongoing balancing act with the colonial powers forced Chulalongkorn to make room for change and modernity, whereas Bhumibol's kingship, at greater remove from political power, squarely rested on classic Buddhist legitimacy. Surviving eighteen *coups d'état* and living through sixteen changes of the constitution, Bhumibol was presented as a friendly 'pillar of stability' rather than as an active ruler. Increased distance from daily politics can turn monarchy into a beacon of harmony and at the same time ensure its survival—a pattern demonstrated most spectacularly by the Japanese emperors.

With improved infrastructures and media technologies, the theatre of royalty was broadcast on ever larger scales everywhere. Victoria and Francis-Joseph have been described as media-monarchs watched by eager audiences in churches, streets, and squares. Photography and moving images brought further change. Who could have expected the excited coverage of royal deaths, births, and marriages in our times? What attracts multitudes to these occasions and glues others to the screen? Rather than subsiding, the fairy-tale mystique of dynasty has expanded to include celebrity stars in many fields, from sport heroes and pop icons to the Hollywood scene. Surprisingly, Twitter, Facebook, and

Instagram have strengthened the charm of dynasty, and in the end royals may still eclipse the celebrity newcomers.

Autocrats: royal style, nepotism, and succession

In February 1788, James Madison, one of America's 'founding fathers', plausibly presented election and short terms in office as the most effective and appropriate means to prevent the 'degeneracy' of powerholders. Elections would reward distinction and talent, he assumed, rather than hereditary status. Short tenure, moreover, made it possible to replace the incompetent while motivating the successful to remain on the right track. Elections allowed the talented to rise to power and at the same time made room for political disputation. Change could now take shape by the well-ordered replacement of officeholders within a stable form of government. The problem of succession to executive office seemed to have been solved in a thoroughly satisfying way. The degeneracy of kings and the repeated outbreaks of bloody succession strife, so typical for dynastic power, appeared to have been overcome. Notwithstanding this fundamental shift, however, a cursory look at modern politics reveals many characteristics familiar from the long history of dynastic power.

Leaders who come to power through popular election can become autocrats. Nimbly moving from one leading office to another, they amass power, dominate their parties, and acquire control over the security apparatus. When the continuation or alternation of the roles of prime minister and president is prevented by constitutional hurdles, rules can be suspended or changed. Media and the judiciary will be manipulated to disable the opposition. Strong men who grab power through open violence move to a similar position in one stroke.

Modern autocrats hold far more powers than did their traditional dynastic precursors, who never commanded resources on the same scale or level of technology and were usually held in check by elites. As soon as power is concentrated in the hands of one person, some of the appurtenances of royalty follow almost naturally. Authoritarian leaders are prone to widely broadcast their idealized image and often appear as overly heroic royals. Vladimir Putin, restoring Russian national pride as well as consolidating his own position, consciously treads in the footsteps of the Russian tsars. The imposing setting of the Kremlin affords him dynastic grandeur, rendered more personal by the repeated coverage of his outdoor activities and virile physique. Engaging in dialogue with the population in carefully prepared meetings, he uses a familiar combination of royal characteristics: grandeur, strength, justice. Turkish president Recep Tayyip Erdoğan revised the constitution and constructed an imposing new presidential palace in Ankara. Erdoğan, too, places himself in the tradition of his dynastic precursors, the Ottoman sultans. In 2019, during the centenary celebration of Sultan Abdulhamid II's death, he, not unreasonably, underlined continuities between modern Turkey and its imperial-dynastic predecessor. A few days later, in a fuming speech, he challenged critics of Turkish foreign policy by saying that they apparently had 'never got an Ottoman slap in their lives'.

The overbearing power of a single political leader acquires more dynastic traits if it coincides with the rise of kin and in-laws to key positions. The circle of confidants around Putin and Erdoğan includes a limited number of relatives; more visible examples of nepotism strike the eye elsewhere. One observer of modern leaders in the Arabic world noted that 'Bourguiba's son, Qaddafi's cousins, Assad's brother, Saddam's in-laws have all played important roles in the policy-making and security establishments.' These strong men of Tunisia, Libya, Syria, and Iraq respectively were no exception. Dictators, more often than not, use their relatives and confidants to dominate institutions. Much like princely families in the dynastic past, kin and retainers form the nucleus of a web of alliances. Variants of godfather-type structures of power, centred around a patron (boss, *caudillo*) and his family, can be found on all continents and at both extremities of the political spectrum. Notwithstanding his communist pedigree Romanian dictator Nicolae Ceauşescu (1918–89) made his spouse Elena second-in-command and his son Nicu secretary of the parliament; three brothers and several in-laws held key positions in ministries, and more family members led important institutions. Cuban leader Fidel Castro (1926–2016) promoted his brother Raul to become his deputy and successor.

Moving one critical step further, fathers could choose to groom their sons as heirs-apparent, and silently persuade representative bodies to clamour for the son's appointment. Syria's Hafez al-Assad (1930, r. 1971–2000) considered the succession of his brother and his eldest son before turning to his younger son Bashar al-Assad. 'Papa Doc' Duvalier (1907, r. 1957–71) prepared his son 'Baby Doc' (1951, r. 1971–86) to succeed him as president-for-life of Haiti. In the case of the sequence of Somoza presidents of Nicaragua (r. 1937–79), succession moved from father to two sons before the regime collapsed. Personality cult, nepotism, and the designation of a successor can be found in many cases: only rarely, however, does hereditary succession in modern republics reach the third generation. This makes North Korea an exception: with Kim Il-sung (1912, r. 1948–94), Kim Jong-il (1941, r. 1994–2011), and Kim Jong-un (1983, r. 2011–present) hereditary rule now comprises three generations.

The persistence in power of the Kim family makes dynastic patterns more conspicuous. On 13 February 2017, Kim Jong-un's half-brother Kim Jong-nam (see Figure 10) was assassinated. After holding senior responsibilities in the North Korean government, this eldest son and most likely successor of Kim Jong-il lost favour. Henceforth, Kim Jong-nam's erratic, lifestyle, and increasingly critical stance towards his successful younger half-brother turned him into a liability. He performed a familiar dynastic role: the rogue half-brother who besmears the

10. Kim Jong-nam: a boy groomed for power? (*Time*, 24 February 2017, 'The Despotic Dynasty: A Family Tree of North Korea's Kim Clan').

ruler's reputation and might still pose a threat. The scramble for the throne of half-brothers had been a common feature of the polygynous dynastic past, and fratricide a frequent practice of victorious kings. Few rulers serenely accepted the manipulations of surviving competitors at other courts. In February 1495, after a peregrination lasting more than a decade, Sultan Cem, half-brother of the Ottoman Sultan Bayezid II (1447, r. 1481–1512), died in suspect circumstances in Italian exile. Examples of assassination, imprisonment, and mutilation can be added *ad libitum*.

The trial and execution of leading statesman Jang Song-thaek in December 2013 brings to mind another familiar dynastic fixture. Jang was the husband of Korea's founding father Kim Il-sung's only daughter and had become the power behind the throne in the latter days of second-generation leader Kim Jong-il.

For third-generation Kim Jong-un the predecessor's favourite was an unwelcome leftover, raising doubts about his personal authority. The ascent of a new prince commonly coincided with a major overhaul of top echelons of office holders. Favourites, in particular, faced violent downfall after the death of their patron: prolonging in power the favourite of an elderly predecessor inevitably undermined the new ruler's credibility. Ottoman history again offers a parallel case: Grand Vizier Sokollu Mehmed Pasha (1506–79) started his tenure under one sultan, became the dominant political player under the next sultan, whose daughter he married, and was assassinated early in the reign of the third sultan, Murad III, who was probably involved in the plot.

In 2018, finally, the series of breakthroughs in the relationship between North Korea and the United States was initiated by the visit of Kim Jong-un's sister Kim Yo Jong to the Pyeongchang Olympic Winter Games. Dynastic women typically served as intermediaries: they could make a first tentative move without compromising their male relative's towering prestige.

Political families: power begets power

Autocrats across the globe have shown a remarkable disposition to mimic forms of dynastic representation, promote their families, and designate their own successors. Yet the dynastic impulse is not limited to the world of modern dictators. 'Political families', with elected representatives and dignitaries in every generation, figure in most stable modern democracies. Elections organize competition for short-term high office, yet competitors can be re-elected and can move on from one assembly to another, or to executive office. The long-standing service and visibility of a senior politician can facilitate the rise to power of his sons or daughters. Consequently, political families with a history of successfully vying for power have appeared in most democracies. An authority on American political families stated that 'political nobility is as American as apple pie'. From the early days of the

Republic until the 20th century, scions of the Adams family held public office. Shortly after its 1848 arrival in the United States the Kennedy family reached high office; it would become the most conspicuous political dynasty during the later 20th century. The flamboyant lifestyles of several family members contributed to the Kennedy mystique, and the tragic murders of President John Kennedy and presidential candidate Robert Kennedy definitively enshrined the family in popular imagination. Family appointments, ubiquitous in autocratic regimes, can also be found in democracies. Following his election in 1960, John F. Kennedy quickly promoted his brother Robert to the office of Attorney General, the youngest incumbent of that office since 1814. Donald Trump started his presidency in 2016 with a conspicuous role for his daughter Ivanka and her spouse Jared Kushner, and in some respects appeared to run his administration as a private business.

The upper echelon of famous American national 'dynasties' comprises fewer than twenty families, yet at the local level, many others can be added. Looking beyond tenure in office, the marriage alliances and networks of these families strike the eye: this is family enterprise in politics. A recent calculation suggests that the dynastic factor in American representative assemblies declined from an average of 11 per cent until 1858 to 7 per cent after 1966; it also shows that the presence of political families has been stronger in the Senate than in the House.

The US example is far from exceptional. Most democracies include families who combine repeated electoral success with tenure in executive office—mayors, governors, ministers, and leading civil servants. European democracies count numbers of political families, notably also at the regional level. Patricians and nobles continued their sway from the early modern age into the early 20th century, seeking alliances with leading business interests and new families. In post-war Europe their names will still be found in assemblies and in high office, though numbers have decreased. Asian democracies such as India, Japan, South

Korea, Thailand, Indonesia, and the Philippines show heredity in more conspicuous form. In the Thai elections held between 1975 and 2018, 42.8 per cent of all MPs hailed from political families. Second- and third-generation 'hereditary politicians' (*seshu giin*) occupy more than 25 per cent of the seats in the Japanese House of Representatives. Heredity is also strong in the bureaucracy and in executive government office. Current prime minister Shinzo Abe can boast a long family tradition matching that of other families such as Fukuda and Hatoyama.

Why do families re-appear in power, notwithstanding the fact that the ultimate rewards can be obtained only through election and mostly in short-term office? In an August 2000 interview, presidential candidate George W. Bush reflected that 'Dynasty means something inherited...you don't inherit a vote. You have to win a vote. We inherited a good name, but you don't inherit a vote'. Bush's rejoinder was correct, but it failed to acknowledge the very substantial advantages of families in power. Their names are familiar to the electorate, they rely on established parties and networks of supporters, they often command substantial wealth, and they can acquire financial support more easily than newcomers. Undeniably, there is no individual heredity in office, neither can there be a guarantee of political success. Nevertheless, 'power begets power': families will cultivate their role in public office and imbue their scions with family mores and examples of forebears. The admixture of high office, public renown, networks, and the dynastic sense of *noblesse oblige* connects modern political families to their pre-modern precursors.

There is a remarkable story to be told about women, political office, and the impact of heredity. In the past, royal blood enabled women in certain circumstances to rise to power in spite of the strong preference for male rule. Pedigree still helps women to overcome gender bias. Women representatives in modern democracies more often come from political dynasties than their male colleagues. In the US, '31.2 % of women legislators are dynastic vs. 8.4% of men'. The rise of the percentage of women elected to representative assemblies during recent decades in Thailand and India, on closer inspection, also reflects a surge of the dynastic element in politics. During the elections in 2004, 2009, and 2014 in India percentages of chosen candidates from political families averaged 20 per cent for men against 55 per cent for women. Since 1975, a remarkable 70 per cent of Thai women MPs could boast a family background in politics.

More striking still is the strong presence of male politicians' widows. In the post-war US, spouses of deceased politicians with a long record of service stood a good chance of being chosen in their stead; as in earlier times, widowhood opened doors that otherwise remained closed. Globally, much the same can be said about women in supreme office. A recent study lists only twenty-seven women among the 1,941 rulers of 20th-century independent countries; a more restricted and precise estimate counts 108 women in power between 1960 and 2015. Such scores do not seem to stray far from pre-modern times; moreover, they hide another echo of dynasty. Among the women who rose to supreme power between 1960 and 1995, a remarkable 50 per cent were preceded in office by their husbands or fathers. Sirimavo Bandaranaike of Sri Lanka became the world's first female prime minister after the violent death of her husband in 1959; Indira Gandhi and Benazir Bhutto became prime ministers of respectively India and Pakistan after the violent deaths of their fathers.

The legacy of assassination could give rise to very different styles of female leadership. Indira Gandhi, member of a powerful political dynasty and groomed for the task by her father Jawaharlal Nehru, was known for her tough style of governing. She ranks among those ruling women whose force of character disposes some in their environment to label them as 'iron ladies'—a group including women without any dynastic associations, with Golda Meir and Margaret Thatcher as notable examples. Widows were more often projected onto the political stage unexpectedly and without preparation. Their political role was founded on their exceptional position as a woman and an outsider. Corazon Aquino, who became the embodiment of Philippine opposition after the violent death of her husband Benigno, always underlined her reluctance to enter the fray. Countering President Marcos's derogatory remarks about her inexperience, she confirmed that she lacked experience in 'cheating, stealing, lying, or assassinating political opponents'. Violetta Chamorro, who took over her murdered husband's newspaper and later became president of Nicaragua, told the electorate: 'I am not a politician, but I believe this is my destiny. I am doing this for Pedro and for my country'. These diverging ways to deal with the clash between femininity and power echo the strategies as well as the perception of ruling women in pre-modern times. Queen-mothers could wield power under the mantle of motherly care and mercifulness; sovereign queens energetically accepting the burdens of power were more likely to inspire sneers about their masculine style of behaviour.

Dynastic enterprise

Ruling houses persist in changed conditions, autocrats almost inevitably take on some of the appurtenances of dynastic power, and politicians beget politicians. Yet perhaps the closest modern parallels of dynastic practice can be found in family businesses. In the domain of public government family power is equated with nepotism and corruption; heredity in power is frowned upon. There is no such widely shared reservation against family-owned and family-managed companies. Moreover, few would argue against the legitimacy of the transmission of wealth and property from one generation to another.

Family businesses were long regarded as reflecting a stage in the development of modern economies, relevant mostly for small-scale enterprise and in developing countries. Recent appraisals stress the lasting role of family businesses in economies around the world, in small companies as well as in major conglomerates. The share of family companies in the gross domestic product stands at 10 per cent or higher in all countries. Seventeen family-led businesses rank among the hundred leading companies in the US and Germany. For Italy, Spain, and Portugal the figures are far higher. Asian family corporations have long been dominant: in modern Japan successors of the pre-war *zaibatsu* family conglomerates persist in reduced form; the South Korean *chaebol*, notably Hyundai, are another example of family-directed conglomerates. Family businesses are not restricted to certain sectors of the economy. Families active in the automobile industry (Ford, Toyoda, Agnelli/Fiat) and in banking (Rothschild, Morgan, Barings) have attracted particular attention, yet other families have made their way in clothing and cosmetics, agriculture, beverages, sweets, furniture, and tyres (Levi Strauss, L'Oréal, Cargill, Heineken, Ferrero, Ikea, Michelin).

In some respects, family companies diverge from their non-family competitors. As long as the family maintains its coherence, family-led businesses have the advantage of rapid decision-making. Moreover, they often define longer-term goals, taking distance from the increasing emphasis on immediate benefits common in modern corporate culture, exacerbated by the expectation of bonuses for successful managers and windfall profits for shareholders. However, the predominance of a family also brings multiple risks: generation change and sibling conflicts can wreak havoc. The long-term view, moreover, might entail conservative, risk-avoiding investment policies. A manager-owner combines the twin responsibilities of leading the family and the company. In both capacities choices are required, and the priorities of the family can diverge from company interests. The head of the family needs to strike a balance between different groups and clashing interests—a predicament typical for royalty.

Leading a family company raises a panoply of dynastic issues. Even in the modern world, formal laws regarding family and inheritance leave many choices about the rights of relatives to the wealth generated by a company. Concentration of rights in a small group creates have-nots and therefore foments rivalry within the family; sharing rights with an inflating group of relatives may undermine the company and in the long run reduce family status. These dilemmas immediately bring to mind dynastic variants of succession and the policies vis-à-vis supernumerary princes.

Succession remains the Achilles' heel of all dynastic constructions: can it proceed smoothly, and allow an advantageous position to family members while doing justice to the qualities of the candidates? Turbulent phases of changeover, with a dominant founding figure unwilling to step down even at an advanced age and a pushy son or daughter, or even multiple relatives competing for leadership, can ruin firms. Preparing the ground for a generational transition is a major challenge for family firms: it has all the potential for father–son drama and sibling rivalry familiar from dynastic history. Founder Henry Ford dominated and humiliated his son and successor Edsel, a drawn-out case of 'parental oppression'.

Which members of the family can take an active part in the leadership of the firm? Any major company, much like kingdoms in the past, needs the experience and talent of outsiders: firms hiring incompetent relatives to perform sinecures, or worse, jumble serious tasks, will have a hard time keeping afloat. Training and experience are indispensable for ambitious family scions who face the competition of outside candidates. Over time, the family almost necessarily becomes less dominant, with outsiders being recruited in executive office and a reduced family presence among stockholders. The individual leadership of a founder can metamorphose into more institutionalized and collegial forms of management in the second or third generations—a development we have seen in many consolidating kingdoms. Finally, families can be removed altogether from day-to-day leadership, reaping the benefits of their business from a distance, or acting as benevolent mascots during infrequent board meetings, where they endorse choices prepared by others. It is no coincidence that the most enduring family companies have followed these paths.

Withdrawing from the day-to-day leadership, family leaders could retain substantial symbolic importance and boost family continuity as well as the firm's success, somewhat like the remarkably enduring Japanese imperial house. In 1868 the Japanese Meiji Emperor re-emerged on the political scene, ending a long period of rule by Shoguns. Business scions, too, can return to active control of the family firm after a long phase of management by outsiders. William Clay Ford Jr., the great-grandson of founder Henry Ford and the product of a second-generation marital alliance with the Firestone family, became Ford's chief executive officer in 2001, sixteen years after the retirement of his uncle Henry Ford II.

Are daughters eligible for executive office as well as ownership? Notwithstanding women's suffrage and emancipation, the traditional dynastic preference for sons long persisted in the world of family businesses: women rose to executive office infrequently, and have only recently come to the fore as fully eligible successors. Typically, the marriage of daughters to executive officers connected these outsiders to the family interest; alternatively, their marriages cemented alliances with other leading families. With the gradually increasing presence of women among business executives, marriage alliances will work in both ways, for men and women. Overall, women in companies have been important for ensuring family relations, continuity, and cohesion. Before they themselves became eligible for executive office, they acted as go-betweens, arranged family alliances, and were the main conduits of family values. With the addition of religion and charity, this was the portfolio of their dynastic predecessors.

The longevity of family businesses cannot be taken for granted. Much like usurpers and warlords, only a minority of business leaders can pave the way for their descendants. Among the myriads of small firms starting as family initiatives only 30 per cent reach a second generation, and a mere 10 per cent survive into the third generation. Yet family businesses pass this critical threshold far more often than autocrats or families in elected office. Longer-term processes of change therefore are more easily visible here than among political dynasties. The Nobel-prize-winning novel by Thomas Mann, *Buddenbrooks*, about the Lübeck-based Buddenbrook grain merchants, became emblematic for the rise and fall of business families. Mann painted a modern variant of the dynastic cycle, with a resolute down-to-earth founder and his straightforward son, succeeded by a talented but complicated grandson. This third-generation head of the house, the main character of the novel, led the business to unprecedented heights, but at the same time sowed the seeds of decay. His success and sophistication inspired admiration—yet he was consumed by doubts and anxieties, worsened by clashes with his sickly son, who cared more for music than for the family company. Endless variants of Mann's gripping story can be found in literature as well as in reality. Scions of families known for business leadership preferred science or the arts to the vocation of their forefathers. Others might be intimidated by the conspicuous example of their predecessors and lose confidence, or simply escape the burdens by squandering family wealth in a life of luxury and extravagance.

This powerful image of generational decline does not always match practice, but as in most clichés, there is a grain of truth. The labours and dedication of the founder, his proximity to the world of the workers, and astonishing rise from rags to riches are documented in many stories. These tales bring us back to the simplicity and purity underlined by Ibn Khaldun and found in the

Chinese tradition of the dynastic cycle. Korean Hyundai's founder Chung Yu-yung reported

> my father was known in his whole village to be the hardest-working man, and my mother never stopped working, making home-spun fabrics. Their actions told us to be diligent and hard-working. My father was a man of few words. I cannot recall receiving any praise from him when I was small.

In their turn, the founder's sons underlined that their father, too, was a towering figure, making all decisions single-handedly, and inspiring obedience through his personal charisma rather than by bullying.

Perhaps business families need a founding story, motivating them to stick to the right track in order to contradict the expectation that shirtsleeves will return to shirtsleeves in three generations. A collection of letters written by family business owners to their successors reads like the moral catalogues compiled by—or ascribed to—dynastic founders for posterity. We recognize injunctions to stay true to the founder's dreams and family values: maintain the quality of products, a staunch loyalty to the shop floor, and trustworthiness vis-à-vis clients. Advice is permeated by the need to ensure family cohesion and the perceived risk of decline through moral erosion, hubris, and internal squabbles. After relating in glowing terms the winning combination of her parents, the second-generation leader of one company gives her children a 'magic formula: stay together'. Writing at the critical point of the dynastic cycle, she exhorts the third generation to preserve 'togetherness'. The same term has been used to translate the Ibn Khaldunian idea of 'asabiyya', group feeling: the quality that was expected to dissolve in the third generation. Remarkably, the advice literature for managers contains numerous injunctions that could have been copied from the literature on the good prince: be true to friends, listen to outside advisors, consult with your kin, select words carefully, exert self-control, and discipline your impulses, never make ill-considered promises but always honour pledges. These winning formulae are usually presented as reflecting the founders' attitudes and activities. It is more plausible to see them as aspiring standards for all generations, perhaps particularly hard to live up to for children who grow up in wealth, removed from the concerns of other social groups.

Epilogue

Wealth, learning, and power can be obtained by talent and toil, but family background makes an immense difference. Throughout history, elites have developed instruments to consolidate the status of their families, by enlarging their patrimony, educating their scions, and seeking strategic alliances. Modern elites in all spheres of life conform to this rule, though heredity of supreme political office is now no longer commonly accepted. Traditional dynasties have disappeared into the margins of politics, yet the dynastic impulse persists, and there is little reason to assume that it will diminish.

Separated from sovereignty, constitutional monarchs can still perform some ideals of traditional kingship—standing above the parties and acting as a focus of unity. Paradoxically, these aspirations can be reached more easily by figures isolated from executive power and everyday political bargaining. Royal interventions can have an impact as long as they meticulously avoid partisan attitudes and are phrased in elusive language: an echo of pre-modern advice literature. The persistence of Japanese imperial dignity suggests that staying above the fray was always the best chance for dynasties to retain their symbolic supremacy. To some extent, this holds true for modern royals, yet, like their pre-modern precursors, they need to cope with conflicting demands. Reducing the public presence to a handful of carefully choreographed moments may long have been acceptable for the Japanese emperor; it clashes with popular expectations in most constitutional monarchies. Royals need to exude cordiality as well as dignity. Mixing with people heightens the stakes: a swarm of royalty watchers, sycophantic in most of their reporting, eagerly jump on any hint of conflict or scandal—common occurrences in most families, and more likely where the stakes are high. The balance between reticence and involvement, and the need to maintain order in the family, thoroughly familiar from the past, still define the strengths and the vulnerabilities of modern constitutional monarchy.

Whether or not dynasties lose their thrones, their long history offers a series of lessons about personalized settings of power. The abstraction of the modern state, much like the fiction of absolute royal sovereignty, always hides a jumble of persons and interests. The ideological cleavage separating two centuries of post-revolutionary history from the preceding millennia has helped to obscure lasting features of persons in power. Too often, the dynastic muddle has been used largely to highlight the achievements of modern political leadership. This book does not deny the dynastic record of violent manipulation and blundering ineptitude, but it places it in the context of pre-modern ideals and standards. In our age, power holders assert profoundly different ideals, yet practices show remarkable persistence. Mao's personal physician stated about his former master that 'the intrigues in China's ancient imperial courts were a far more powerful influence on his thought than Marxism-Leninism.' As soon as leaders hold power for a longer time or develop authoritarian traits, they will find themselves in a position matching in some respects that of their predecessors on the throne. Consciously or unknowingly, they will replicate some of the strategies of dynastic rulers. They can choose to copy the splendour of royalty, populate the corridors of power with stalwarts and relatives, and even seek to groom preferred sons for supreme power. Early 21st-century history, finally, strongly suggests that the language of strong men and conspicuous family power still has the capacity to enthral populations. The preceding pages allow readers to reconsider such phenomena from the long-term perspective of dynastic power.

References

Dynasties past and present

Chinghua Tang, *The Ruler's Guide: China's Greatest Emperor and His Timeless Secrets of Success* (Stroud 2017).
Sixteen million Chinggisids. Tatiana Zerjal et al., 'The Genetic Legacy of the Mongols', *The American Journal of Human Genetics*, 72 (2003) figure at 720.

Chapter 1: Shaping the family

'Poor men were monogamists all over the world'. Miriam Koktvedgaard Zeitzen, *Polygamy: A Cross-Cultural Analysis* (Oxford; New York 2008) 14.
Akbar's wives. Jeroen Duindam, *Dynasties: A Global History of Power 1300–1800* (Cambridge 2016) 112.
Battle between priests and warriors. Georges Duby, *Le chevalier, la femme et le prêtre: le mariage dans la France féodale* (Paris 1981).
Erasmus on war and marriage. Erasmus, 'The Marriage Alliances of Princes', *Education of a Christian Prince* (many editions).
Changing patterns of inheritance among European nobles. Paula Sutter Fichtner, *Protestantism and Primogeniture in Early Modern Germany* (New Haven 1989); David Warren Sabean, Simon Teuscher, Jon Mathieu, *Kinship in Europe: Approaches to Long-Term Development (1300–1900)* (New York 2007); Hamish Scott, *Forming Aristocracy: The Reconfiguration of Europe's Nobilities, c.1300–1750* (Oxford forthcoming 2020).

'A branch can get so heavy that it breaks the trunk; a tail can get too big to be wagged'. Denis Twitchett, 'How to Be an Emperor: T'ang T'ai-tsung's Vision of His Role', *Asia Major*, 3rd Series, 9 (London 1996) 1–102 at 58–63.

Chapter 2: Paterfamilias: it's hard to be the boss

'Sun of the city of Babylon, who spreads light over the lands of Sumer and Akkad'. Dominique Charpin, '"I am the Sun of Babylon". Solar aspects of Royal Power in Old Babylonian Mesopotamia', in Jane A. Hill, Philip Jones, and Antonio J. Morales (eds.), *Experiencing Power, Generating Authority: Cosmos, Politics, and the Ideology of Kingship in Ancient Egypt and Mesopotamia* (Philadelphia 2013) 65–96 at 65.

'Like a fly in the toils of a spider, could hardly stir a limb for the threads of custom'. J. G. Frazer, *The Golden Bough* (New York; London, 1894) I, 209–10.

'To make justice prevail…'. Martha T. Roth, *Law Collections from Mesopotamia and Asia Minor* (Atlanta 1997) 134–4; see also 76 and other references.

'I annihilated enemies…'. Martha T. Roth, *Law Collections from Mesopotamia and Asia Minor* (Atlanta 1997) 133.

'Gentleness causes oppression…'. James Gray, *Ancient Proverbs and Maxims from Burmese Sources: Or The Niti Literature of Burma* (London 1886) 92.

'Power tends to corrupt…'. E. E. Dalberg Acton, 'Acton–Creighton correspondence', in Gertrude Himmelfarb (ed.), *Essays on Freedom and Power* (London 1956) 335–6.

'What is the meaning…'. Jonathan Spence, *Emperor of China. Self-Portrait of Kang-Hsi* (New York 1974) 134.

Yongjo and Sado. JaHyun Kim Haboush, ed., *The Memoirs of Lady Hyegyong: The Autobiographical Writings of a Crown Princess of Eighteenth-Century Korea* (New York 1996).

'If an ordinary man…'. Chinghua Tang, *The Ruler's Guide: China's Greatest Emperor and His Timeless Secrets of Success* (Stroud 2017) 12.

'Silence is double security…'. Reuben Levy (ed. and trans.), *A Mirror for Princes: The Qabus Nama by Kai Ka'us Ibn Iskandar prince of Gurgan* (London 1951) 41.

'Don't cause trouble with my tongue…'. Willem-Frederik van Nassau-Dietz, *Gloria Parendi. Dagboeken van Willem Frederik*

*stadhouder van Friesland, Groningen en Drenthe 1643–1648,
1651–1654*, ed. J.Visser and G. N. van der Plaat (The Hague 1995)
May 1644, 43.

'Speaking a lot . . .'. Charles Dreyss (ed.), *Mémoires de Louis XIV pour
l'instruction du Dauphin*, I–II (Paris 1860) I, 195–7; II, 64–5.

'we shall see . . .'. Louis de Rouvroy duc de Saint-Simon, *Mémoires*, ed.
A. de Boislisle (Paris 1916) XXVIII, 45–6, 143–6.

'Be silent as though in a drunken stupor . . .'. Burton Watson, *Han Fei
Tzu: Basic Writings* (New York 1964) 19.

'Sing him a song of "Placebo"'. Francis Bacon, 'Of Counsel', *The Essays*,
ed. John Pitcher (London 1985) 120–4 at 124.

'Employs men as a skilled carpenter . . .'. Chinghua Tang, *The Ruler's
Guide: China's Greatest Emperor and His Timeless Secrets of
Success* (Stroud 2017) 18.

'The jealousy of one . . .'. Charles Dreyss (ed.), *Mémoires de Louis
XIV pour l'instruction du Dauphin*, I–II (Paris 1860) II, 267.

Chapter 3: Women and dynastic power

'Wept copiously', 'Seventeen of his brothers'. C. E. Bosworth, *History
of al-Tabari*. Vol. 5: *The Sasanids, the Byzantines, the Lakhmids,
and Yemen* (New York 1999) 398.

'His relatives all fought for the throne . . .'. Stefan Amirell, 'The
Blessings and Perils of Female Rule: New Perspectives on the
Reigning Queens of Patani, c. 1584–1718', *Journal of Southeast
Asian Studies*, 42, 2 (2011), 307.

'Buran, restorer . . .'. Touraj Daryaee, *Sasanian Persia: The Rise and
Fall of an Empire* (London; New York 2009) 36.

'Never will succeed such a nation as makes a woman their ruler'.
Al-Bukhārī, Abū 'Abd Allāh Muḥammad b. Ismā'īl, *Kitāb al-Jāmi'
al-Ṣaḥīḥ*, ed. L. Krehl and Th. W. Juynboll, 4 vols. (Leiden
1862–1908) IV, 376–7. See a translation at https://sunnah.com/
bukhari/92/50.

'Ancestral custom'. Pamphili Eusebius, *Ecclesiastical History,
Books 1–5: Fathers of the Church, a New Translation* (New York
1953) 87.

'A masculine sort of woman . . .'. Strabo, *Geography of Strabo, Book
XVII & General Index* (Cambridge, MA; London 1932) 139.

Gudit of Ethiopia. Knud Tage Andersen, 'The Queen of the Habasha
in Ethiopian History, Tradition and Chronology', *Bulletin of the
School of Oriental and African Studies*, lxiii (2000) 40.

'Are you saying…'. Keith McMahon, 'Women Rulers in Imperial China', *NAN NÜ*, xv (2013) 191.

Chapter 4: Embedding the family

Iyasu's Locket. Henry Arrowsmith-Brown, ed., *Prutky's Travels to Ethiopia and Other Countries* (London 1991) 99, 172.

Süleyman's war helmet and 'Sultan of the worlds'. Gülru Necipoglu, 'Süleyman the Magnificent and the Representation of Power in the Context of Ottoman–Hapsburg–Papal Rivalry', *The Art Bulletin*, lxxi (1989); Rachel Milstein, 'King Solomon or Sultan Süleyman?', *The Ottoman Middle East: Studies in Honor of Amnon Cohen* (Leiden; Boston 2013).

'The Prime Minister…'. Jean-Baptiste Tavernier, *The Six Voyages of John Baptista Tavernier Through Turkey Into Persia and the East-Indies, Finished in the Year 1670: Together with a New Relation of the Present Grand Seignor's Seraglio, by the Same Author* (London 1678) 221.

'When a viper bit a eunuch…'. Constantine Manasses cited in Paul Magdalino, 'In Search of the Byzantine Courtier: Leo Choirosphaktes and Constantine Manasses', in H. Maguire (ed.), *Byzantine Court Culture from 829 to 1204* (Washington, DC 1997) 163.

Divide-and-rule. Norbert Elias, *The Court Society* (Oxford 1983 [1969]) took this as point of departure for his explanation of royal power, the 'royal mechanism' or 'Königsmechanismus'.

Chapter 5: Persistence and change

'Mere hollow show'. Sima Qian, *Records of the Historian; Chapters from the Shih Chi of Ssu-Ma Ch'ien*, Burton Watson, Kametarō Takigawa, ed. (New York 1969) 118; Burton Watson, *Ssu-Ma Ch'ien: Grand Historian of China* (Taipei 1975).

'No dynasty lasts beyond the lifespan of three generations'. Ibn Khaldun, *The Muqaddimah. An Introduction to History*, ed. Franz Rosenthal (Princeton; Oxford 1967) 136–8.

'Humility and respect'. Ibn Khaldun, *The Muqaddimah. An Introduction to History*, ed. Franz Rosenthal (Princeton; Oxford 1967) 106.

Zhu Yuanzhang's concerns about his sons' wrongdoings. Hok-Lam Chan, 'Ming Taizu's Problem with His Sons: Prince Qin's Criminality and Early-Ming Politics', *Asia Major* 20, 1 (2007) 87.

'Unnecessary between humans, and reserved for God alone'. Haus- Hof- und Staatsarchiv Wien, Ältere Zeremonialakten, K 9130 X 1786, Joseph II's personal note to Starhemberg.

Chapter 6: The dynastic impulse in the modern world

'Holocaust of crowns'. Churchill used the expression in his 1934 essay 'a holocaust of crowns' in his 'Will the world swing back to monarchies?', in M. Wolff (ed.), *The Collected Essays of Sir Winston Churchill* (London 1976) IV, 269.

Measures against the 'degeneracy' of power holders. James Madison, 'The Federalist 57'.

'Ottoman slap'. 'Turkey Opens the Door to Exiled Ottoman Royals', *The Times*, 13 February 2018, https://www.thetimes.co.uk/article/turkey-brings-ottoman-heirs-in-from-the-cold-n0ddzqsh2 and 'Turkish President Erdogan offers US "Ottoman slap" ahead of Rex Tillerson's visit to Turkey', *The Independent*, 15 February 2018, https://www.independent.co.uk/news/world/middle-east/turkey-us-president-erdogan-rex-tillerson-ottoman-slap-visit-secretary-state-a8212731.html

'Bourguiba's son, Qaddafi's cousins...'. Lisa Anderson, 'Absolutism and the Resilience of Monarchy in the Middle East', *Political Science Quarterly*, cvi (1991) 11.

'Political nobility is as American as apple pie'. Stephen Hess, *America's Political Dynasties from Adams to Clinton* (Washington DC 2016) quote on back flap.

Numbers of 'dynastic' members in US assemblies. Stephen Hess, *America's Political Dynasties from Adams to Clinton* (Washington DC 2016): 6%; Ernesto Dal Bó, Pedro Dal Bó, and Jason Snyder, 'Political Dynasties', *The Review of Economic Studies*, lxxvi (2009) 119: 7%.

'Dynasty means something inherited...'. 'My heritage is part of who I am': interview with George W. Bush by Walter Isaacson, CNN/*Time*,

http://edition.cnn.com/ALLPOLITICS/time/2000/07/31/heritage.html

'31.2 % women legislators are dynastic vs. 8.4% of men'. Pedro Dal Bó, and Jason Snyder, 'Political Dynasties', *The Review of Economic Studies*, lxxvi (2009) 119, 132.

Dynastic women in Thai politics. Yoshinori Nishizaki, 'New Wine in an Old Bottle: Female Politicians, Family Rule, and Democratization in Thailand', *The Journal of Asian Studies*, lxxvii (2018); Amritu

Basu, 'Women, Dynasties, and Democracy in India', in Kanchan Chandra, *Democratic Dynasties* (Cambridge 2017).

Women in supreme office. Arnold M. Ludwig, *King of the Mountain: The Nature of Political Leadership* (London 2013) 22, 435; Farida Jalalzai, 'Global Trends in Women's Executive Leadership', in Verónica Montecinos, ed., *Women Presidents and Prime Ministers in Post-Transition Democracies* (London 2017) 60.

Aquino and Chamorro quotes respectively in M. R. Thompson and C. Derichs (eds.), *Dynasties and Female Political Leaders in Asia: Gender, Power and Pedigree* (Berlin 2013) 156; Michael A. Genovese and Janie Steckenrider (eds.), *Women as Political Leaders: Studies in Gender and Governing* (New York 2013) 125.

Average presence of family businesses in GDP. Andrea Colli, *The History of Family Business, 1850–2000* (Cambridge; New York 2003), 27.

'Parental oppression'. G. Gordon and N. Nicholson, *Family Wars: Classic Conflicts in Family Business and How to Deal with Them* (London 2008) 99–104.

See the stages discussed in John L. Ward, *Perpetuating the Family Business: 50 Lessons Learned from Long-Lasting, Successful Families in Business* (Basingstoke 2004).

Generations and survival. Wendy C. Handler, 'Succession in Family Business: A Review of the Research', *Family Business Review*, 7, 2 (1994) 133.

'My father was known in his whole village…'. Donald Kirk, *Korean Dynasty: Hyundai and Chung Ju Yung* (London; New York 1994) 5–6, 21–2.

'Magic formula: stay together'. D. Kenyon-Rouvinez et al., *Sharing Wisdom, Building Values: Letters from Family Business Owners to their Successors* (New York 2011) 28, 12–13.

Epilogue

'The intrigues in China's ancient imperial courts…'. Zhisui Li, *The Private Life of Chairman Mao: The Memoirs of Mao's Personal Physician* (London 1994) 122–4 quote at 124.

Further reading

Chronologies and genealogies of ruling families throughout history can be found, usually with a strong emphasis on larger and longer-lasting kingdoms and empires of Europa and Asia; see for example:

John E. Morby, *Dynasties of the World: A Chronological and Genealogical Handbook* (Oxford; New York 2018).

Online resources such as Wikipedia provide lists of royalty for all periods and places, including all examples mentioned in this book.

Succession, kinship, royal clans (Chapter 1)

David Murray Schneider and Kathleen Gough, *Matrilineal Kinship* (Berkeley 1962). Explains some of the basics of matrilineal descent.
Jack Goody (ed.), *Succession to High Office* (Cambridge 1966). This edited volume includes a powerful introduction by Goody, whose numerous publications on families and forms of descent and inheritance have been very influential.
Rubie S. Watson and Patricia B. Ebrey (eds.), *Marriage and Inequality in Chinese Society* (Berkeley; Los Angeles 1991). An important collection including chapters on imperial clans as well as general comparative discussions of family, marriage, and inheritance.
John W. Chaffee, *Branches of Heaven: A History of the Imperial Clan of Sung China* (Cambridge, MA 1999). An exemplary study of one Chinese imperial clan.
Macabe Keliher, 'The Problem of Imperial Relatives in Early Modern Empires and the Making of Qing China', *The American Historical*

Review 122, 4 (2017) 1001–37. Includes relevant comparative observations.

Robert Bartlett, *Blood Royal: Dynastic Politics in Medieval Europe* (Cambridge, forthcoming 2020) provides an authoritative overview of dynastic themes in medieval Europe with numerous quotes from primary sources.

David Warren Sabean, Simon Teuscher, and Jon Mathieu, *Kinship in Europe: Approaches to Long-Term Development (1300–1900)* (New York 2007). A recent initiative that restores kinship as an important factor in European history.

Few works have dealt with the combination of kingship, dynasty, and the royal court outlined in this VSI. A more detailed examination, considering a more limited period but with an extensive bibliography and footnotes guiding the reader towards numerous regional studies is:

Jeroen Duindam, *Dynasties: A Global History of Power 1300–1800* (Cambridge 2016).

Kingship (Chapter 2) has a long-standing and coherent bibliography, based first and foremost on a series of classics examining its sacred dimensions

J. G. Frazer, *The Golden Bough* (New York; London, 1894). An important and wide-ranging work focusing on the sacrality of kings.

Marc Bloch, *The Royal Touch: Sacred Monarchy and Scrofula in England and France* (Montreal 1973 [Paris 1924]). Elaborating the most familiar sacred aspect of European kingship.

Arthur M. Hocart, *Kingship* (London 1927). One among several works by the same author outlining shared properties of kings, including an attempt at the comparison of coronations.

Ernst Kantorowicz, *The King's Two Bodies: A Study in Mediaeval Political Theology* (Princeton, NJ 1957). An influential study describing the conceptual separation between undying kingship and the mortal incumbent.

Two prominent works have considered, from very different angles, the political nature and impact of royal power:

Karl August Wittfogel, *Oriental Despotism: a Comparative Study of Total Power* (New Haven; London 1957). Triggered by the examples of Nazi and Communist totalitarianism, Wittfogel reconsidered royal and imperial power in history—a work rich in ideas and erudition, but misguided in its overall orientation.

Norbert Elias, *The Court Society* (Oxford 1983 [1969]). A powerful but one-sided analysis of the court of Louis XIV of France, seen as the nemesis of French nobles and as an example of the author's model of civilization as the control of emotions (*Affektbeherrschung*).

More recent discussions of kingship and monarchy

W. M. Spellman, *Monarchies 1000–2000* (London 2001). A descriptive typology of various types of monarchies.

Declan Quigley, *The Character of Kingship* (Oxford 2005). A volume with academic discussions of kingship and sacrality.

Francis Oakley, *Kingship: The Politics of Enchantment* (Oxford 2008). A view focused on religion and kingship mostly in Europe and the Near East.

Marshall Sahlins and David Graeber, *On Kings* (Chicago 2017). A masterful synthesis by two powerful scholars, at times high-handed and inaccessible.

Alan Strathern, *Unearthly Powers: Religion and Politics in World History* (Cambridge 2019). Wide-ranging comparative examination of changing forms of religion, kingship, and conversion.

Women and power; queenship (Chapter 3)

Anne Walthall (ed.), *Servants of the Dynasty: Palace Women in World History* (Berkeley; Los Angeles 2008). With a strong introduction by the editor and a wide sweep of cases.

Clarissa Campbell-Orr (ed.), *European Queenship: The Role of The Consort 1660–1815* (Cambridge 2004).

Keith McMahon, *Women Shall Not Rule: Imperial Wives and Concubines in China from Han to Liao* (Lanham 2013). Presents many individual cases but notably includes general and comparative observations on polygyny and gender roles.

Leslie P. Peirce, *The Imperial Harem: Women and Sovereignty in the Ottoman Empire* (Oxford, 1993).

Barbara Watson Andaya, *The Flaming Womb: Repositioning Women in Early Modern Southeast Asia* (Honolulu, 2008).

Stefan Amirell, 'Female Rule in the Indian Ocean World (1300–1900)', *Journal of World History*, xxvi (2016).

Royal courts and representations of dynastic power (Chapter 4)

Norbert Elias, *The Court Society* (Oxford 1983 [1969]) still is an important starting point.

David Cannadine and Simon Price (ed.), *Rituals of Royalty: Power and Ceremonial in Traditional Societies* (Cambridge 1987).

John Adamson (ed.), *The Princely Courts of Europe: Ritual, Politics and Culture under the Ancien Régime, 1500–1750* (London 2000).

Jeroen Duindam, *Vienna and Versailles. The Courts of Europe's Dynastic Rivals* (Cambridge 2003).

Antony Spawforth (ed.), *The Court and Court Society in Ancient Monarchies* (Cambridge 2011).

Evelyn Rawski, *The Last Emperors: A Social History of Qing Imperial Institutions* (Berkeley; London 1998). A masterful and detailed examination of the Qing court and Qing rule.

Modern monarchies, political families, and business dynasties (Chapter 6)

Stephen Hess, *America's Political Dynasties from Adams to Clinton* (Washington, DC 2016).

David Landes, *Dynasties: Fortunes and Misfortunes of the World's Great Family Businesses* (New York 2006).

Kanchan Chandra, *Democratic Dynasties* (Cambridge 2017).

Andrea Colli, *The History of Family Business, 1850–2000* (Cambridge; New York, 2003).

M. R. Thompson and C. Derichs, *Dynasties and Female Political Leaders in Asia: Gender, Power and Pedigree* (Berlin 2013).

Thomas Mann, *Buddenbrooks: The Decline of a Family*. Powerful literary examination of the generations of a declining business family.

Index

A

Abbas I, Safavid Shah 37
Abbasid caliphate 54–5, 64
  servants 74
Abdulhamid II, Ottoman
  Sultan 102–3
Abe, Shinzo 107–8
abolition of monarchy 94–5
Abomey palace 71
Abu'l Fazl 13–14
Aceh (Indonesia), female
  rulers 44–5, 50
Acton, Lord 33
Adams, American political
  family 106–7
adoption of successors 16, 51
advisors of kings 38–41
Africa 65–6
  courts and palaces 71–2
  female rulers 45–6
  kingmakers 9–10
  matrilineal succession 7
  patrilineal succession 8
  polygamy 14–15
  queen-mothers 53–4
  reign mates 53–4,
    58–9, 99
  sacredness of kings 26
  succession rights 21–2

Ahmed I, Ottoman Sultan 51–2
Ain Jalut, battle of 64
Akbar, Mughal Emperor 13–14
al-Assad, Hafez and Bashar 104
Al-Tabari 43
Alawi dynasty, Morocco 98
Alexander the Great 62, 87
Ali, Fourth Caliph 62–4
America
  conquest 92–3
  elections 102
  political families 106–8
  republicanism 96–7
Anne of Austria, French Queen-
    Mother and Regent 51–2
anthropology 2–3
antiroyalism 28
approaches to the study of
    dynasty 2–3
Aquino, Corazon 109–10
Arab countries, nepotism 103–4
Arab Spring (2010–12) 98
Arabian Peninsula 97–8
archaeology 2–3
Aristotle 5, 83–4
art history 2–3
Arwa, Queen of Yemen 47
Asante federation 7–9, 15
  reign mates 53–4
  stool 27–8

K

Kaikavus, Ziarid Prince 39
Kangxi, Qing Emperor 36–7
Kavad II, Sasanian King 43
Kedarite Arab tribal federation 45–6
Kennedy, American political family 106–7
Khosrow I, Sasanian King 83
Khosrow II, Sasanian King 43
Khurram, Mughal Prince 77
Kim family, North Korea 104–6
Kim Jong-nam 104–5
kingdoms
    established in 19th century 96
    established in the 20th century 97
kingmakers 9–10
kings 1–2
    abolition of monarchy 94–5
    adapting to change 100–1
    advisors of 38–41
    authority 28
    children as 34–6
    cosmic connections 24–5
    diplomacy 32–3
    divine powers 27
    elderly 37–8
    as judges and lawmakers 30–2, 39–40, 79
    killing of 25–6, 43, 86–7
    longevity 34–7
    mistresses 57–8
    moral supremacy 29–30
    morality 33
    as objects of ceremony 27–8
    people's expectations 29–34
    performing sacrifices and ceremonies 75–81
    polygamous see polygamy
    polygynous see polygyny
    reign mates 53–4, 58–9, 99
    relationships with successors 36–7
    responsibilities 24
    royal courts 70–4
    sacredness 25–9, 90–1, 93
    training manuals or 'mirrors' for 38–9
    trust in others 38
    value of silence 40
    wives and concubines 54–7
kinglists 82–3
Knox, John 50
Korea 36–7
    end of dynastic rule 97
    female rulers 45–6
    Kim family 104–6
    North 104–6
    South 110–11
Kösem Sultan, Ottoman Sultan-Mother 15, 51–3
Kush 53
    female leaders 45–6, 50–1

L

lawmakers, kings as 30–2, 39–40, 79
Leopold I, Habsburg Emperor 35–6
Liao dynasty 87
Libya, republic 98
Louis Bonaparte, Napoleon's brother 96
Louis IX, King of France 30–2
Louis XIII, King of France 22–3, 52–3
Louis XIV, King of France (Sun King) 22–5, 35–6, 39–41, 57–60
    court 71–2
Louis XVI, King of France 27, 30–2, 94–5
Lovedu (South Africa) 11–12
    rain queens 45–6

M

Machiavelli, Niccolò 9–10, 33, 38
Madison, James 102

Index

AFRICAN HISTORY
A Very Short Introduction
John Parker & Richard Rathbone

Essential reading for anyone interested in the African continent and the diversity of human history, this *Very Short Introduction* looks at Africa's past and reflects on the changing ways it has been imagined and represented. Key themes in current thinking about Africa's history are illustrated with a range of fascinating historical examples, drawn from over 5 millennia across this vast continent.

'A very well informed and sharply stated historiography...should be in every historiography student's kitbag. A tour de force...it made me think a great deal.'

Terence Ranger,
The Bulletin of the School of Oriental and African Studies

www.oup.com/vsi